Armenian Poems

Rendered Into English Verse

By Alice Stone Blackwell

PANTIANOS
CLASSICS

Published by Pantianos Classics

ISBN-13: 978-1-78987-538-6

First published in 1917

Contents

Preface

Two considerations led to the publication of this book. The first was the belief that the sympathy felt for the Armenians in their unspeakable sufferings at the hands of the Turks would be deepened by an acquaintance with the temper and genius of the people, as shown in their poetry.

The second was the fact that Armenian poetic literature, while well worthy to be known, was practically inaccessible to English-speaking readers. Its treasures are locked up in an almost unknown language.

Each of these translations in verse has been made from a literal translation in prose, furnished to me in English or French by my Armenian friends. Among those who rendered this help were the late Mr. Ohannes Chatschumian of Leipzig University, Professor Minas Tchéraz of King's College, London, editor of "L'Arménie;" the late Kevork Tourian, the martyred Bishop of Trebizond: Archag Tchobanian, Garabed H. Papazian, Haroutune Asian, Arsen Diran, Avedis B. Selian, Sahag Chuchian, Aram Torossian, Karekin Manoukian, O. H. Ateshian, Arshag D. Mahdesian, editor of "The New Armenia," Bedros A. Keljik and D. K. Varzhabedian.

The poems that make up the first part of this volume were published by Roberts Brothers in 1896. They were well received, as the press comment in the Appendix will show. The book has been long out of print. This new and enlarged edition has been privately printed.

Alice Stone Blackwell.

3 Monadnock Street, Dorchester, Mass.

Introduction

ARMENIAN poetry is so full of allusions to Vartan, Avarair, Haig, and Thorkom or Togarmah, as well as to the Garden of Eden, that a few preliminary notes are necessary by way of explanation.

Armenia is a mountainous region of Western Asia, lying around Mount Ararat, and containing the sources of the Tigris, Euphrates, and Araxes rivers. It is south of the Caucasus Mountains, between the Black, Caspian, and Mediterranean seas. According to tradition, it was the site of the Garden of Eden.

Armenia was the seat of one of the most ancient civilizations of the globe. Its people were contemporary with the Assyrians and Babylonians. They are of Aryan race, and of pure Caucasian blood.

Their origin is lost in the mists of antiquity. According to their own tradition, they are the descendants of Thorkom, or Togarmah, a grandson of Japhet, who settled in Armenia after the Ark rested on Ararat; They call themselves Haik, and their country Haiasdan, after Haig, the son of Togarmah. one of their greatest kings. In the earliest days of recorded history, we find them occupying their present home. They are referred to by Herodotus. Xenophon describes their manners and customs much as they still exist. In the Bible it is mentioned that the sons of Sennacherib escaped "into the land of Armenia." Ezekiel also refers to Armenia, under the name of Togarmah, as furnishing Tyre with horses and mules, animals for which it is still famous; and "the Kingdom of Ararat" is one of the nations summoned by Jeremiah to aid in the destruction of Babylon.

Tradition relates that Christianity was preached in Armenia early in the first century, by the Apostles Thaddeus and Bartholomew. It is historic fact that in A. D. 276 the king and the whole nation became Christian, under the preaching of Saint Gregory, called "the Illuminator." The Armenian Church is thus the oldest national Christian church in the world.

As a Christian nation whose lot has been cast beyond the frontiers of Christendom, the Armenians have had to suffer constant persecution, — in early times from the Persian fire-worshippers, in later centuries from the Mohammedans. Since the withdrawal of the Crusaders, to whom they alone of Asiatic nations gave aid and co-operation, the Armenians have been at the mercy of the surrounding heathen peoples. Their country has been invaded successively by the Caliphs of Bagdad, the Sultans of Egypt, the Khans of Tartary, the Shahs of Persia, and the Ottoman Turks. All these invasions were accompanied by fierce persecutions and great barbarities; but the Armenians have held tenaciously to their faith for more than fifteen hundred years.

In the middle of the fifth century Armenia had already lost its national independence. It was ruled by feudal chiefs and princes who were subject to the King of Persia. The Persians at this time were aiming at the conquest and conversion of the world. In A. D. 450 the Persian King sent a letter to the Armenian princes, setting forth the excellence of fire-worship and the foolishness of Christianity, and formally summoning Armenia to embrace fire-worship. A great council was called, in which bishops and laymen sat together, and a reply of unanimous refusal was drawn up. Eghiché, an Armenian historian of the fifth century, one of the bishops who signed the refusal, has preserved in his history the text of this remarkable document. First they answered at considerable length the arguments of the Persian King against Christianity. In conclusion they said: —

"From this faith no one can move us, — neither angels nor men; neither sword, nor fire, nor water, nor any deadly punishment. If you leave us our faith, we will accept no other lord in place of you; but we will accept no God in place of Jesus Christ: there is no other God beside him. If, after this great confession, you ask anything more of us, lo, we are before you, and our lives are in your power. From you, torments; from us, submission; your sword, our necks. We are not better than those who have gone before us, who gave up their goods and their lives for this testimony."

The King of Persia was as much amazed as enraged by the boldness of this reply; for Armenia was a small country, and stood alone, without allies, against the vast power of Persia. A Persian army of 200,000 men was sent into Armenia. The battle was fought on the plain of Avarair, under Mount Ararat. The much smaller force of the Armenians was defeated, and their leader, Vartan, was killed. But the obstinate resistance offered by rich and poor — men, women, and children — convinced the King of Persia that he could never make fire-worshippers of the Armenians. As the old historian quaintly expresses it, "The swords of the slayers grew dull, but their necks were not weary." Even the high-priest of fire saw that the Persians had undertaken an impossibility, and said to the Persian King: —

"These people have put on Christianity, not like a garment, but like their flesh and blood. Men who do not dread fetters, nor fear torments, nor care for their property, and, what is worst of all, who choose death rather than life, — who can stand against them?"

This battle was the Armenian Marathon, and the national songs are full of allusions to it. To-day, after fifteen hundred years, the mountaineers of the Caucasus, at their festivals, still drink the health of Vartan next after that of the Catholicos, or head of their church. From time immemorial it has been the custom in Armenian schools to celebrate the anniversary of the battle with songs and recitations, and to wreathe the picture of Vartan with red flowers. Of late years this celebration has been forbidden by the Russian and Turkish governments.

In the minds of the common people, all sorts of picturesque superstitions still cluster around that battlefield. A particular kind of red flowers grow there, that are found nowhere else, and it is believed that they sprang from the blood of the Christian army. A species of antelope, with a pouch on its breast secreting a fragrant musk, is supposed to have acquired this peculiarity by browsing on grass wet with the same blood. It is also believed that at Avarair the nightingales all sing, "Vartan, Vartan!"

The Armenians, according to their own histories and traditions, enjoyed four periods of national independence, under four different dynasties, extending over about 3,000 years. The ruins of Ani and other great cities still testify to their former power and splendor. It is now many centuries, however, since they lost their political independence; and their country has been little more than a battle-ground for rival invaders. Armenia, an Asiatic Poland, was long ago divided between Russia, Persia and Turkey.

By Article 61 of the Treaty of Berlin, in 1878, the Armenians in Turkey were placed under the protection of the European powers; but the jealousy of the powers among themselves has prevented any effective protection from being given. There were frightful massacres of the Armenians in 1894-96 by order of the Sultan Abdul Hamid. In 1908, the Armenians, in common with the other subject nationalities in Turkey, enjoyed a brief time of sunshine when constitutional government was proclaimed; but the old oppressions soon began again, and they culminated in the unparalleled cruelties of 1915-16. It is not necessary here to go into the harrowing details; they have been spread broadcast in the press.

The excuse put forward by the Turks — the claim that there was a dangerous Armenian revolution impending — was a mere pretext. Turkish oppression was such that it would have justified a revolution a thousand times over, if there had been any chance of success; but there was none. The Turks knew it; most of the Armenians knew it; and therefore the Patriarch of Constantinople and the representative Armenians in Turkey disapproved of the revolutionary propaganda that was carried on by some of the younger men, mainly in America and Europe. Only a handful of the Armenians in Turkey had anything to do with it. And this was made the pretext for giving the men of a whole nation over to slaughter, and the women to outrage and starvation!

It was no outburst of popular fanaticism, but a coldly premeditated crime, carried out by orders from Constantinople, ruthlessly and systematically, as a political measure. In the midst of the massacre, when a Red Cross nurse begged a high Turkish official to spare the children, his answer was, "Women have no business to meddle in politics!"

And what kind of people were thus given over to destruction? Dr. James L. Barton, secretary of the American Board of Foreign Missions, and former president of Euphrates College in Turkey, says:

"I know the Armenians to be, by inheritance, religious, industrious and faithful. They are the Anglo-Saxons of Eastern Turkey. They are not inferior in mental ability to any race on earth. I say this after eight years' connection with Euphrates College, which has continually from 550 to 625 Armenians upon its list of students, and after superintending schools which have 4,000 more of them."

The Hon. Andrew D. White says: "It is one of the finest races in the world, physically, morally and intellectually. If I were asked to name the most desirable races to be added by immigration to the American population, I would name among the very first the Armenian."

Lord Bryce says: "They are a strong race, not only with vigorous nerves and sinews, physically active and energetic, but also of conspicuous brain power. Among all those who dwell in Western Asia they stand first, with a capacity for intellectual and moral progress, as well as with a natural tenacity of will and purpose, beyond that of all their neighbors — not merely of Turks, Tartars, Kurds and Persians, but also of Russians.

"Thus they have held a very important place among the inhabitants of Western Asia ever since the sixth century. If you look into the annals of the East Roman or Byzantine Empire, you will find that most of the men who rose to eminence in its service as generals or statesmen during the early middle ages were of Armenian stock. So was it also after the establishment of the Turkish dominion in Europe. Many of the ablest men in the Turkish service have been Armenians by birth or extraction. The same is true of the Russian service."

Lamartine calls the Armenians "the Swiss of the East." Dulaurier compares them to the Dutch.

Mrs. Isabella Bird Bishop, the famous traveler, says: "They are the most capable, energetic, enterprising and pushing race in Western Asia, physically superior and intellectually acute, and, above all, they are a race which can be raised in all respects to our own level...Their shrewdness and aptitude for business are remarkable, and whatever exists of commercial enterprise in Asia Minor is almost altogether in their hands."

After teaching among them for thirty-five years, Dr. Cyrus Hamlin wrote: "The Armenians are a noble race." Dr. Grace N. Kimball, who lived for years in the heart of Armenia, calls them "a race full of enterprise and the spirit of advancement, much like ourselves in characteristics, and full of possibilities of every kind." So says the Rev. Frederick D. Greene, who was born and brought up among them.

Miss Florence E. Fensham, Dean for years of the American College for Girls at Constantinople, told me that she had found the Armenian girls among her students not only able, but very faithful and trustworthy.

H. F. B. Lynch says: "The Armenian people may be included in the small number of races who have shown themselves capable of the highest culture."

Speaking of the importance of spreading Western progressive ideas in the East, he says:

"In the Armenians we have a people who are peculiarly adapted to be the intermediaries of the new dispensation. They profess our religion, are familiar with some of our best ideals, and assimilate each new product of European culture with an avidity and thoroughness which no other race between India and the Mediterranean has given any evidence of being able to rival. These capacities they have made manifest under the greatest disadvantages...

"If I were asked what characteristics distinguish the Armenians from other Orientals, I should be disposed to lay most stress on a quality known in popular speech as *grit*. It is this quality to which they owe their preservation as a people, and they are not surpassed in this respect by any European nation. Their intellectual capacities are supported by a solid foundation of character, and, unlike the Greeks, but like the Germans, their nature is averse to superficial methods; they become absorbed in their tasks and plumb them deep...These tendencies are naturally accompanied by forethought and balance; and they have given the Armenian his pre-eminence in commercial affairs. He is not less clever than the Greek; but he sees farther."

Rev. Edwin M. Bliss says, with truth: "Those who know the race most widely and most intimately esteem it the most highly."

Mrs. Julia Ward Howe, who was president of the Friends of Armenia, wrote:

"Some Americans have been prejudiced against Armenians by contact with the demoralized Armenians of Constantinople. But in Constantinople corruption extends to all nationalities. Ubicini draws a very just distinction between the Armenians of Constantinople and the Levantine ports and the Armenians of Tauris or Erzcrum, the cradle of the race, where the independent and chivalrous character of the people has remained comparatively little changed by the lapse of ages. The contrast is as great as between the enervated Greeks of Phanar and the hardy Greek mountaineers of Epirus and Macedonia. The bulk of the Armenians are primitive and hard-working agriculturists, living in the interior, and what Lord Byron said of them years ago holds good to-day: 'It would perhaps be difficult to find in the annals of a nation less crime than in those of this people, whose virtues are those of peace, and whose vices are the result of the oppression it has undergone.'"

When the recent terrible events began, the Armenians who could fled over the frontier. Refugees by hundreds of thousands are crowded together in Russia, in Egypt, in Greece, destitute of everything, and perishing like flies. The need is desperate, and on a colossal scale. Contributions for the relief fund should be sent to Charles R. Crane, 70 Fifth Avenue, New York City.

Part I

Little Lake

Bedros Toukian, the son of an Armenian blacksmith of Scutari, was born in 1851. He lived in great poverty, and died of consumption in 1872. He left a number of dramas and poems that enjoy a great popularity among his countrymen.

Why dost thou lie in hushed surprise,
  Thou little lonely mere?
Did some fair woman wistfully
  Gaze in thy mirror clear?

Or are thy waters calm and still
  Admiring the blue sky,
Where shining cloudlets, like thy foam,
  Are drifting softly by?

Sad little lake, let us be friends!
  I too am desolate;
I too would fain, beneath the sky,
  In silence meditate.

As many thoughts are in my mind
  As wavelets o'er thee roam;
As many wounds are in my heart
  As thou hast flakes of foam.

But if heaven's constellations all
  Should drop into thy breast,
Thou still wouldst not be like my soul, —
  A flame-sea without rest.
There, when the air and thou are calm,

The clouds let fall no showers;
The stars that rise there do not set,
  And fadeless are the flowers.

Thou art my queen, O little lake!
  For e'en when ripples thrill
Thy surface, in thy quivering depths
  Thou hold'st me, trembling, still.

Full many have rejected me:
  "What has he but his lyre?"
"He trembles, and his face is pale;
  His life must soon expire!"

None said, "Poor child, why pines he thus."
  If he beloved should be,
Haply he might not die, but live, —
  Live, and grow fair to see."

None sought the boy's sad heart to read,
  Nor in its depths to look.
They would have found it was a fire,
  And not a printed book!

Nay, ashes now! a memory!

Grow stormy, little mere,
For a despairing man has gazed
Into thy waters clear!

Wishes for Armenia

When bright dews fall on leaf and flower,
And stars light up the skies,
Then tears and sparks commingled
Burst forth from my dim eyes.
Forget thee, O Armenia!
Nay, rather may I be
Transformed into a cypress dark.
And so give shade to thee!

The starry sky no comfort brings:
To me it seems a veil
Strewn with the tears that Ararat
Sheds from his summit pale.
O graves! O ruins! to my soul
Your memory is as dear
As to the lover's thirsting heart
The maiden's first love-tear.
And shall my spirit after death
Oblivious be of you?
Nay, but become a flood of tears.
And cover you with dew!

Not sword nor chains, abysses deep
Nor precipices fell,
Not thunder's roll, nor lightning's flash,
Nor funeral torch and knell —
Not all of these, 'neath death's dark stone
Can ever hide from me
The glowing memories of the past,
Our days of liberty.

Forget you? Ne'er will I forget,
O glorious days of yore!
Rather may I be changed to fire
And bring you back once more!

When twinkle pale the stars at dawn,
When dewy buds unclose,
And tenderly the nightingale
Is singing to the rose,
All Nature's harmonies, alas!
Can ne'er give back to me
The sighs that sound where cypress boughs
Are moaning like the sea.
Forget you, black and bitter days?
No, never! but instead
Rather may I be turned to blood,
And make your darkness red!

Armenia's mountains dark may smile,
Siberia's ice may smoke,
But stern, unbending spirits still
Press on my neck the yoke.
Inflexible and cold are they;
When feeling surges high,
And I would speak, they stifle down
My free soul's bitter cry.
Forget thee, justice? Never!
But ere my life departs,
Rather may I become a sword,
And make thee pierce men's hearts!

When e'en the rich man and the priest
A patriot's ardor feel.
And when Armenian hearts at length
Are stirred with love and zeal —
When free-souled sons Armenia bears,

These days of coldness past,
And fires of love and brotherhood
　　Are lighted up at last —
Shall I forget thee then, my lyre?
　　Ah, no! but when I die
Rather may I become thy voice,
　　And o'er Armenia sigh!

To Love

A galaxy of glances bright,
　　A sweet bouquet of smiles,
A crucible of melting words
　　Bewitched me with their wiles!

I wished to live retired, to love
　　The flowers and bosky glades,
The blue sky's lights, the dew of morn,
　　The evening's mists and shades;

To scan my destiny's dark page,
　　In thought my hours employ,
And dwell in meditation deep
　　And visionary joy.

Then near me stirred a breath that seemed
　　A waft of Eden's air.
The rustle of a maiden's robe,
　　A tress of shining hair.

I sought to make a comrade dear
　　Of the transparent brook.
It holds no trace of memory;
　　When in its depths I look.
I find there floating, clear and pale,
　　My face! Its waters hold

No other secret in their breast
　　Than wavelets manifold.

I heard a heart's ethereal throb;
　　It whispered tenderly:
"Dost thou desire a heart?" it said.
　　"Beloved, come to me!"

I wished to love the zephyr soft
　　That breathes o'er fields of bloom;
It woundeth none, — a gentle soul
　　Whose secret is perfume.

So sweet it is, it has the power
　　To nurse a myriad dreams;
To mournful spirits, like the scent
　　Of paradise it seems.

Then from a sheaf of glowing flames
　　To me a whisper stole:
It murmured low, "Dost thou desire
　　To worship a pure soul?"

I wished to make the lyre alone
　　My heart's companion still.
To know it as a loving friend.
　　And guide its chords at will.

But she drew near me, and I heard
　　A whisper soft and low:
"Thy lyre is a cold heart," she said,
　　"Thy love is only woe."

My spirit recognized her then;
　　She beauty was, and fire,
Pure as the stream, kind as the breeze,

And faithful as the lyre.

My soul, that from the path had erred,
  Spread wide its wings to soar,
And bade the life of solitude
  Farewell forevermore.

A galaxy of glances bright,
  A sweet bouquet of smiles,
A crucible of melting words
  Bewitched me with their wiles!

New Dark Days

The centuries of bloodshed
  Are past, those cruel years;
But there is still one country
  Whose mountains drip with tears.
Whose river-banks are blood-stained.
  Whose mourning loads the breeze, —
A land of dreary ruins,
  Ashes, and cypress-trees.

No more for the Armenian
  A twinkling star appears;
His spirit's flowers have faded
  Beneath a rain of tears.
Ceased are the sounds of harmless mirth.
  The dances hand in hand;
Only the weapon of the Koord
  Shines freely through the land.

The bride's soft eyes are tearful.
  Behind her tresses' flow,
Lest the Koord's shout should interrupt
  Love's whisper, sweet and low.

Red blood succeeds love's rosy flush;
  Slain shall the bridegroom be,
And by the dastard Koords the bride
  Be led to slavery.

The peasant sows, but never reaps;
  He hungers evermore;
He eats his bread in bitterness,
  And tastes of anguish sore.
Lo! tears and blood together
  Drop from his pallid face;
And these are our own brothers,
  Of our own blood and race!

The forehead pure, the sacred veil
  Of the Armenian maid,
Shall rude hands touch, and hell's hot breath
  Her innocence invade?
They do it as men crush a flower,
  By no compunction stirred;
They slaughter an Armenian
  As they would kill a bird.

O roots of vengeance, heroes' bones.
  Who fell of old in fight,
Have ye all crumbled into dust,
  Nor sent one shoot to light?
Oh, of that eagle nation
  Now trampled by the Koord,
Is nothing left but black-hued crows,
  And moles with eyes obscured?

Give back our sisters' roses,
  Our brothers who have died.
The crosses of our churches,
  Our nation's peace and pride!

O Sultan, we demand of thee
  And with our hearts entreat —
Give us protection from the Koord,
  Or arms his arms to meet!

What Are You, Love?

What are you, love? A flame from heaven?
  A radiant smile are you?
The heaven has not your eyes' bright gleams,
  The heaven has not their blue.

The rose has not your snowy breast;
  In the moon's face we seek
In vain the rosy flush that dyes
  Your soft and blushing cheek.

By night you smile upon the stars,
  And on the amorous moon,
By day upon the waves, the flowers —
  Why not on one alone?

But, though I pray to you with tears,
  With tears and bitter sighs,
You will not deign me yet one glance
  Cast by your shining eyes.

O love, are you a mortal maid,
  Or angel formed of light?
The spring rose and the radiant moon
  Envy your beauty bright;

And when your sweet and thrilling voice
  Is heard upon the air,
In cypress depths the nightingale
  Is silent in despair.

Would I, a zephyr, might caress
  Your bright brow's dreams in sleep,
Breathe gently on your lips, and dry
  Your tears, if you should weep!

Or would that in your garden fair
  A weeping rose I grew;
And when you came resplendent there
  At morning with the dew,

I'd give fresh color to your cheek
  That makes the rose look pale.
Shed on your breast my dew, and there
  My latest breath exhale.

Oh, would I were a limpid brook!
  If softly you drew nigh,
And smiled into my mirror clear,
  My blue waves would run dry.

Oh, would I were a sunbeam bright,
  To make you seem more fair,
Touching your face, and dying soon
  Amid your fragrant hair!

But, if you love another,
  His gravestone may I be!
Then you would linger near me,
  Your tears would fall on me;

Your sighs would wander o'er me,
  Sighs for his early doom.

To touch you, O beloved,
  I must become a tomb!

I Have Loved Thee

It was the hour of dew and light;
  In heaven a conflagration cold
Of roses burned, instead of clouds;
  There was a rain of pearls and gold.

Then deep within a flowering grove
  I saw thee, love, reclined at ease,
And thou wast languishing and pale,
  And sighing like a summer breeze,

Plucking a blossom's leaves apart
  With fingers fair as lilies are;
Thine eyes, the temples of love's fire,
  Were fixed upon the heavens afar.

I marvelled that thy fingers soft,
  Wherein the haughty rose was pressed,
Had power to pluck her leaves away
  And scatter them upon thy breast.

A strange new heaven shone within
  Thine eyes, so dark and languishing;
A heaven where, instead of stars,
  Arrows of fire were glittering.

Ah, thou hast made of me a slave
  To one bright glance, one word of thine!
The rays thy soul sheds, cruel maid,
  Become as fetters laid on mine.
Oh, leave my heart, from me depart!
  I for my queen desire not thee;

Thy breast is like the rose's leaf,
  Thy heart as granite hard to me.

Thou knowest naught, thou fragrant one,
  Save wounds in tender hearts to make,
Happy when thine adorer's breast
  Bleeds in profusion for thy sake.

When, lonely in a grove's deep shade,
  I weep, and all my sad heart grieves,
Lo, thou art there! Thou findest me.
  Thou speakest to me through the leaves.

When in the swift and shining stream
  I seek oblivion of thy face,
Thou findest me, and from the waves
  Thou smilest up with witching grace.

When to the rocks and mountains steep
  To break my heart and lyre I flee.
Thou murmurest ever in the wind
  That thou hadst never love for me.

I will embrace the frozen earth.
  And hide from thee in dreamless sleep.
The dark grave is a virgin too:
  Is any other heart so deep?

In Memoriam of Vartan Lutfian

Our two devoted hearts were joined and
bound
  By streaming rays, with heaven's own light
aglow;
We read each other's souls like open books,

19

Where 'neath each word lay depths of love
and woe.

Dost thou remember, on Mount Chamlajà,
  In the dark cypress shade where mourners
sigh,
How we two mused, and watched the Bos-
phorus,
  Stamboul's blue girdle, and the cloudless
sky?

We sat in silence; any uttered word
  Would but have marred our souls' infinity.
There like two flames we burned without a
sound,
  And shone upon each other, pale to see.

Like sad black moths that haunt the cypresses,
  Our souls drank in the shadow and the
gloom,
Drank endless sorrow, drank the dark-hued
milk
  Of hopelessness and of the silent tomb.

Deeply we drank, and long; but thou didst
drain
  The darksome cup that to thy lips was
given.
Till thou wast drunken with it, and became
  Thenceforth a pale and silent son of heav-
en.

Thy paleness grieved my soul; thy last faint
look,
  Turned on me ere thy spirit did depart,
Has fixed forevermore, O friend beloved,

The memory of thee in my aching heart.

Oh, art thou happy or unhappy there?
  Send me a message by an angel's wing!
Tedious, alas! and weary is this world,
  Mother of griefs and bitter sorrowing.

If in that world there is a shady tree,
  And a clear brook that softly murmurs
near;
If there are found affection and pure love,
  If the soul breathes a free, fresh atmos-
phere

This very day would I put off this life.
  This poor soiled garment should to dust
return.
Ah. Vartan, answer! In the unknown land,
  Say, hast thou found the things for which I
yearn?

She

Were not the rose's hue like that which glows
  On her soft cheek, who would esteem the
rose?

Were not the tints of heaven like those that
lie
  In her blue eyes, whose gaze would seek
the sky?

Were not the maiden innocent and fair,
  How would men learn to turn to God in
prayer?

Little Gifts

She was alone. I brought a gift —
  A rose, surpassing fair;
And when she took it from my hand
  She blushed with pleasure there.

Compared with her, how poor and pale
  The red rose seemed to be!
My gift was nothing to the kiss
  My lady gave to me.

My Grief

To thirst with sacred longings,
  And find the springs all dry,
And in my flower to fade. — not this
  The grief for which I sigh.

Ere yet my cold, pale brow has been
  Warmed by an ardent kiss,
To rest it on a couch of earth. —
  My sorrow is not this.

Ere I embrace a live bouquet
  Of beauty, smiles and fire,
The cold grave to embrace. — not this
  Can bitter grief inspire.

Ere a sweet, dreamful sleep has lulled
  My tempest-beaten brain.
To slumber in an earthy bed. —
  Ah, this is not my pain.
My country is forlorn, a branch
  Withered on life's great tree;

To die unknown, ere succoring her, —
  This only grieveth me!

Complaints

This poem and the next were written on successive days, a short time before Tourian's death.

Farewell to thee, O God, to thee, O sun,
Ye twain that shine above my soul on high!
My spirit from the earth must pass away;
I go to add a star to yonder sky.

What are the stars but curses of sad souls, —
Souls guiltless, but ill-fated, that take flight
To burn the brow of heaven? They only serve
To make more strong the fiery armor bright

Of God. the source of lightnings! But, ah me!
What words are these I speak? With thunder smite,
O God, and shatter the presumptuous thoughts
That fill me, — giant thoughts and infinite,

Thoughts of an atom in the universe.
Whose spirit dares defy its mortal bars,
And seeks to dive into the depth of heaven.
And climb the endless stairway of the stars!

Hail to thee, God, thou Lord of trembling man.
Of waves and flowers, of music and of light!
Thou who hast taken from my brow the rose.

And from my soul the power of soaring flight;

Thou who hast spread a cloud before mine eyes,
And given these deathly flutterings to my heart,
And bidd'st me smile upon thee on the brink
Of the dark tomb, to which I must depart!

Doubtless thou hast for me a future life
Of boundless light, of fragrance, prayer, and praise;
But; if my last breath here below must end
Speechless and mute, breathed out in mist and haze -

Ah, then, instead of any heavenly life
To greet me when my earthly span is o'er.
May I become a pallid lightning flash.
Cling to thy name, and thunder evermore!

Let me become a curse, and pierce thy side!
Yea, let me call thee "God the pitiless!"
Ah me, I tremble! I am pale as death;
My heart foams like a hell of bitterness!

I am a sigh that moans among the sad.
Dark cypresses, — a withered leaf the strife
Of autumn winds must quickly bear away.
Ah, give me but one spark, one spark of life!

What! after this brief, transitory dream
Must I embrace for aye the grave's cold gloom?
God, how dark a destiny is mine!

Was it writ out with lees from the black tomb?

Oh, grant my soul one particle of fire!
I would still love, would live, and ever live I
Stars, drop into my soul! A single spark
Of life to your ill-fated lover give!

Spring offers not one rose to my pale brow,
The sunbeams lend me not one smile of light.
Night is my bier, the stars my torches are,
The moon weeps ever in the depths of night.

Some men there are with none to weep for them;
Therefore God made the moon. In shadows dim
Of coming death, man has but two desires, -
First, life; then some one who shall mourn for him.

In vain for me the stars have written "Love,"
The bulbul taught it me with silver tongue;
In vain the zephyrs breathed it, and in vain
My image in the clear stream showed me young.

In vain the groves kept silence round about,
The secret leaves forbore to breathe or stir
Lest they should break my reveries divine;
Ever they suffered me to dream of her.

In vain the flowers, dawn of the spring, breathed forth
Incense to my heart's altar, from the sod.

Alas, they all have mocked me! All the world
Is nothing but the mockery of God!

Repentance

Yesterday, when in slumber light and chill.
   Drenched in cold sweats, upon my couch I lay,
While on my panting cheeks two roses burned
   And on my brow sat mortal pallor gray, —

Then on my soul, athirst for love, there fell
   My mother's sobs, who wept beside my bed.
When I unclosed my dim and weary eyes,
   I saw her tears of pity o'er me shed.

I felt upon my face my mother's kiss,
   A sacred last remembrance, on death's shore;
All her great sorrow in that kiss was breathed
   And it was I who caused her anguish sore!

Ah, then a tempest rose and shook my soul,
   A storm of bitter grief, that blasts and sears;
Then I poured forth that torrent dark. My God,
   Forgive me! I had seen my mother's tears.

Liberty

Michael Ghazarian Nalbandian was born in Russian Armenia in 1830; graduated at the University of St. Petersburg with the title of Professor; was active as a teacher, author, and journalist; fell under suspicion for his political opinions, and underwent a rigorous imprisonment of three years, after which he was exiled to the province of Sarakov, and died there in 1866 of lung disease contracted in prison. It is forbidden in Russia to possess a picture of Nalbandian: but portraits of him, with his poem on "Liberty" printed around the margin, are circulated secretly.

When God, who is forever free,
   Breathed life into my earthly frame, —
From that first day, by His free will
   When I a living soul became, —
A babe upon my mother's breast,
   Ere power of speech was given to me.
Even then I stretched my feeble arms
   Forth to embrace thee, Liberty!

Wrapped round with many swaddling bands,
   All night I did not cease to weep,
And in the cradle, restless still,
   My cries disturbed my mother's sleep.
"O mother!" in my heart I prayed,
   "Unbind my arms and leave me free!"
And even from that hour I vowed
   To love thee ever. Liberty!

When first my faltering tongue was freed,
   And when my parents' hearts were stirred
With thrilling joy, to hear their son
   Pronounce his first clear-spoken word,
"Papa, Mamma," as children use.
   Were not the names first said by me;
The first word on my childish lips

Was thy great name, O Liberty!

"Liberty!" answered from on high
  The sovereign voice of Destiny:
"Wilt thou enroll thyself henceforth
  A soldier true of Liberty?
The path is thorny all the way.
  And many trials wait for thee;
Too strait and narrow is this world
  For him who loveth Liberty."

"Freedom!" I answered, "on my head
  Let fire descend and thunder burst;
Let foes against my life conspire,
  Let all who hate thee do their worst:
I will be true to thee till death;
  Yea, even upon the gallows tree
The last breath of a death of shame
  Shall shout thy name, O Liberty!"

Days of Childhood

Days of my childhood, like a dream
  Ye fleeted, to return no more.
Ah, happy days and free from care,
  Ye brought but joy in passing o'er!

Then Science came, and on the world
  He gazed with grave, observant looks;
All things were analyzed and weighed,
  And all my time was given to books.
When to full consciousness I woke,
  My country's woes weighed down my
heart.
Apollo gave me then his lyre,
  To bid my gloomy cares depart.

Alas! that lyre beneath my touch
  Sent forth a grave and tearful voice,
Sad as my soul; no single chord
  Would breathe a note that said "Rejoice!"

Ah, then at last I felt, I knew.
  There never could be joy for me,
While speechless, sad, in alien hands,
  My country languished to be free.

Apollo, take thy lyre again,
  And let its voice, amid the groves,
Sound for some man who may in peace
  Devote his life to her he loves!

To the arena I will go,
  But not with lyre and flowery phrase;
I will protest and cry aloud,
  And strive with darkness all my days.

What boots to-day a mournful lyre?
  To-day we need the sword of strife.
Upon the foeman sword and fire, —
  Be that the watchword of my life!

Armenia

*Archbishop Khorène Nar Bey de Lusignan
was a descendant of the last dynasty of Ar-
menian kings. Nar Bey studied at the cele-
brated convent of the Mechitarists in Venice,
but early left the Roman Catholic for the
Armenian Church. He became an Archbish-
op, and was elected Patriarch of Constanti-
nople, but declined to serve. He was an elo-*

24

quent preacher, and a distinguished poet,
author, and linguist. Nar Bey was a friend of
Lamartine, whose poems he translated into
Armenian. He was one of the Armenian
delegates to the Berlin Congress of 1878. He
died at Constantinople in 1892, poisoned, it
was commonly believed, by the Turkish gov-
ernment, for political reasons.

If a sceptre of diamond, a glittering crown.
Were mine, at thy feet I would lay them both
down,
   Queen of queens, Armenia!

If a mantle of purple were given to me,
A mantle for kings, I would wrap it round
thee,
   Poor Armenia, my mother!

If the fire of my youth and its sinews of steel
Could return, I would offer its rapture and
zeal
   All to thee, my Armenia!

Had a lifetime of ages been granted to me,
I had given it gladly and freely to thee,
   O my life, my Armenia!

Were I offered the love of a maid lily-fair,
I would choose thee alone for my joy and my
care,
   My one love, my Armenia!
Were I given a crown of rich pearls, I should
prize,
Far more than their beauty, one tear from
thine eyes,
   O my weeping Armenia!

If freedom unbounded were proffered to me,
I would choose still to share thy sublime
slavery,
   O my mother, Armenia!

Were I offered proud Europe, to take or re-
fuse,
Thee alone, with thy griefs on thy head,
would I choose
   For my country, Armenia!

Might I choose from the world where my
dwelling should be,
I would say, Still thy ruins are Eden to me,
   My beloved Armenia!

Were I given a seraph's celestial lyre,
I would sing with my soul, to its chords of
pure fire,
   Thy dear name, my Armenia!

The Wandering Armenian to the Cloud

Cloud, whither dost thou haste away
   So swiftly through the air?
Dost thou to some far-distant land
   An urgent message bear?

With gloomy aspect, dark and sad,
   Thou movest on through space;
Dost thou hide vengeance, or has grief
   O'ershadowed thy bright face?

Did a wind come and exile thee
   Far from thy heavenly home,

Like me, in homesickness and tears
   Across the world to roam?

Like me, who wander now, my griefs
   Sole comrades left to me,
While, longing for my fatherland,
   I pine on land and sea?

Cloud, when thy heart is full of tears
   Thou hast relief in rain;
When indignation brims thy breast,
   Fierce lightnings tell thy pain.

Though my heart too is full, my brow
   With painful thoughts oppressed.
To whom can I pour forth the griefs
   That fill an exile's breast?

O cloud, thou hast no native land!
   Far happier thou than I;
To north, to south thou floatest free.
   At home in all the sky.

But I, at every step, shed tears,
   In sadness and in gloom;
Each step away from fatherland
   Is nearer to my tomb!

To My Sister

Fain would I be to thee, my sister sweet,
Like the bright cloud beneath Aurora's feet.
A pedestal to help thee mount on high
Into the blessed peace of the blue sky.
The zephyr would I be, to which is given
To waft the rose's fragrance up to heaven.

That thy pure soul, amid life's stress and
strain,
Might not exhale its perfume sweet in vain.

Fain would I be to thee as crystal dew
Of morn, that doth the young flower's sap
renew.
And with its vapor veils her from the sun,
Lest thy fresh heart be seared ere day is done.

Fain would I be to thee a nightingale,
Telling within thine ear so sweet a tale;
No meaner strain thine eyes with sleep
should dim.
And thou shouldst wake to hear a sacred
hymn.

Fain would I be to thee a broad-armed tree
That casts wide shadow on the sultry lea.
And cheers from far the wandering traveller's
view;
So would my love shed o'er thee shade and
dew.

Fain would I be to thee a refuge sure.
As 'neath the thatch the swallow builds se-
cure.
A humble roof, it yet the rain can ward;
So I from storms thine innocence would
guard.

Ah! when to thee this world, as yet un-
known.
Its barren hopes, its bitterness hath shown,
Fain, fain would I bring comfort in that hour
To thy sad heart. Oh, would I had the power!

Gentle Breeze of Armenia

Where art thou, sweet and gentle breeze,
   Breeze of my fatherland?
The spring has come, and tender flowers
   Bud forth on every hand;
The warm sun smiles upon the world,
   The skies are soft and blue;
Ah, zephyr of Armenia,
   Wilt thou not greet us too?

My country's stars I see no more
   Beneath these alien skies,
And when the radiant spring returns,
   The sad tears fill my eyes.
The sun for exiles has no light,
   Though soft it shine and bland.
Where art thou, oh, where art thou,
   Breeze of my fatherland?

Where art thou, breeze of Ararat?
   Our sad hearts long for thee.
For poplar trees of Armavir
   That whisper pleasantly.
Spring in whose bosom shines no flower
   Sprung from Armenian earth.
To the Armenian is not spring,
   But winter's cold and dearth.

Behold, all Nature calls on us,
   With invitation glad,
To celebrate her victory
   O'er Winter, dark and sad.
The ice has melted, and the flowers
   Awaken and expand;
Where are you, breezes sweet and soft,

Airs of the fatherland?

Out of long, gloomy winters,
   The winters of the past,
Oh, blow for the Armenians,
   And bring us spring at last!
Awake exalted memories
   Of glorious deeds and grand!
Alas, hast thou forgotten us,
   Breeze of the fatherland?

Hast thou forgot our tearful eyes,
   Our bleeding hearts that ache?
Wilt thou not mingle in our griefs.
   Lamenting for our sake?
Why should our sad lyre sob in tears,
   In bitter tears like these,
And thou not come to thrill its chords,
   O soft Armenian breeze?

Oh, from our country's ruins
   Waft to us through the air
Dust of our glorious ancestors,
   Whose bones are buried there!
Life-giving breeze, Armenian breeze
   From distant Edens blown,
Oh, bring to us our fathers' sighs,
   To whisper with our own!

One token bring from home, one drop
   From the Araxes' shore!
Let tears and smiles with memories blend —
   Thoughts of our sires of yore.
Kiss the Armenian's brow and breast;
   Wake patriot ardor bold!
Where art thou, O life-bringing breeze

Our sires inhaled of old?

Power to Armenian cymbals give,
  And in our souls inspire
The zeal of Coghtn's ancient bards,
  Their fervor and their fire!
Imbue Armenian hearts afresh
  With courage firm and true;
Ah, zephyr of Armenia,
  Awake our hope anew!

Let Us Live Armenians

Live as Armenians, brethren, in this world!
  That name to us do history's pages give;
The heavens above salute us by that name:
  Then, brethren, as Armenians let us live!

Armenians we! That hero was our sire
  Who taught mankind for freedom first to
strive; [1]
He gave us for our portion a great name:
  Then, brethren, as Armenians let us live!

Our land is holy; on its sacred soil
  God walked, what time he Adam forth did
drive; [2]
Our language he devised; he spoke it first:
  Then, brethren, as Armenians let us live!

We have one cradle with the human race;
  Our land salvation to the world did give;
Faith's earliest altar was Mount Ararat:
  Then, brethren, as Armenians let us live!

Noble our name is; not on earth alone,

But in the heavens it shines forth gloriously.
The stars of valiant Haig are deathless there:
  Brethren, Armenians let us ever be!

Live as Armenians! From the past what land
  So many ancient glories doth derive?
What nation has so beautiful a home?
  Then, brethren, as Armenians let us live!

Unto what nation did the King of heaven
  Send four apostles as an embassy, [3]
And with what monarch did he correspond?
  Brethren, Armenians let us ever be!

Who can count o'er the names of all our
saints?
  One roll of martyrs is our history;
Our church on earth is like to heaven itself:
  Brethren, Armenians let us ever be!

To us was Christ's first benediction given;
  The champions of the faith for aye were we;
Armenia's deeds astonished earth and heaven:
  Brethren, Armenians let us ever be!

Our nation, ever following the Lord.
  Has borne the cross for many a century;
No, she will not be a deserter now!
  Brethren, Armenians let us ever be!

Yes, sorrowful is life beneath the cross;
  Yes, as Armenians we with pain must strive;
Yet wears the cross the seal of victory:
  Then, brethren, as Armenians let us live!

Our home beloved, our sceptre and our crown.

With clouds are covered in obscurity:
Have hope I the heavens yet shall give us light:
Brethren, Armenians let us ever be!

No, not forever shall our fate be sad,
    Our lot, to eat and drink of misery;
A new and happy future waits for us!
    Brethren, Armenians let us ever be!

Live as Armenians, that our sons as well
    May boast that they are our posterity;
Let us do no dishonor to our name!
    Brethren, Armenians let us ever be!

Live as Armenians! Some day, over death
    Armenia yet shall rise in victory.
Soon may that glad day dawn for us, O heaven!
    Brethren, Armenians let us ever be!

[1] According to tradition, at the time of the building of the tower of Babel, Haig, the ancestor of the Armenians, rebelled against the tyranny of the Assyrian king, and forsook the work with his tribe. The constellation Orion is called by his name in the Armenian language.
[2] Tradition locates the Garden of Eden in Armenia, between the Euphrates and Tigris: and the Armenians believe that their language was spoken by Adam and Eve.
[3] The tradition is that Apgar, King of Armenia, sent messengers to Jesus, entreating him to come and cure the king of a painful malady, and offering to become a Christian. Jesus declined to come, but promised to send some of his apostles after his death who would cure the king. This was done; and Apgar and many of his subjects embraced Christianity.

Let Us Die Armenians

Brothers, we have no hope from foreigners;
    Gaze not around for aid! Though with good-will
The foreigner receive you as a guest,
    He is an alien still.

Unmoved he sees your pain; what matters it
    Although to tears of blood your heart be grieved?
None save Armenians feel Armenia's woes;
    Why are you still deceived?

Rest not upon the foreigner your hope;
    Show not hard eyes your wounds, your deep distress.
Do you then look for sympathy and help?
    They mock your nakedness!

Heavy your burden is, but do you think
    That foreign hands will lift it? You are wrong.
Nay, leave the foreigner, lend brother's arm
    To brother, and be strong!

Fate is your enemy? Be not dismayed.
    But show Armenian hearts, to brave her hate.
Fate cannot vanquish an heroic land
    That battles against fate.

29

Nor swords nor chains could crush the minds and hearts
Of your great ancestors, those valiant ones.
Why are your hearts to-day so weak and faint?
Are you not heroes' sons?

Sons of those matchless heroes who of old
Upon their country's altar bled and died, -
Sons of those great Armenians whose lives
To-day are the world's pride?

Even the mighty nations of the earth
With envy view our nation's history;
Then why, forgetting your past glory, say
To aliens, "Blest are ye"?

Forward! Let him who has an earnest heart
Forsake the stranger, follow his brave sires!
The life of all Armenians centres round
Our faith's clear altar-fires.

Armenia's life shall not become extinct:
The heavens are full of that life-giving flame.
While the all-conquering cross of Christ shall reign,
So long shall live her name.

Why are you fearful? Sec you not. sublime
Above your heads, the shadow of the rood?
Of old your fathers with that sacred sign
Mingled their sacred blood.

Anchor your hope, too, on the cross! Have faith

The light will shine, since you to it are true.
It was your nation's bulwark; be it still
Weapon and flag to you!

A nation that was faithful to the cross
Cannot be lost, though centuries roll past.
While in this world religion shall endure,
Her life shall also last.

In the great names of faith and fatherland,
Clasp hands in love, bid hate and malice flee,
Armenian brothers! Let the nation's foe
Alone accursed be.

Let each heart glow with love for fatherland,
Each mind your country's welfare seek alone;
Let your least brother's pain and tears be felt
As keenly as your own.

Ah! foreign bread can never nourish us,
And foreign water never quench our thirst;
Thou art our life, Armenian font, where we
Received baptism first!

For no vain hope let us deny that font,
Our nation's baptistery! When we yield
Our breath forever, be our place of death
The sacred battlefield!

Let the same earth receive that cradled us;
Armenians we, when life to us was given;
Armenians let us live, Armenians die,
Armenians enter heaven!

They voice thy sighs, and from my heart.
My country, they shall not depart!

A Brave Son of Armenia

There leaned against a gravestone
  Upon a mountain steep,
A fair-haired youth of gallant mien,
  Who mused in sorrow deep.

His eyes now sought the heavens,
  And now the earth below.
Son of the hills and valleys,
  Why dost thou sorrow so?

Dost thou desire, to soothe thee,
  A vast and stormy sea,
Whose ranks of wind-stirred billows
  Shall sing to comfort thee?

Or heaven's immense and wondrous vault.
  Star-strewn, thine eyes to greet?
Or smiles from nature's fairest things.
  The flowers, the zephyrs sweet?
Or dost thou yearn for solace
  All other joys above, —
A gentle mother's kisses,
  A sweetheart's tender love?

To cure thy heart's deep sorrow
  What wouldst thou have, oh, what?
"My longing is for powder.
  For powder and for shot!"

We Are Brothers

From glorious Nature's myriad tongues
  Though songs be breathed by lips of love,
And though the maiden's fingers fair
  Across the thrilling harp-strings rove,
Of all earth's sounds, there is no other
So lovely as the name of brother.

Clasp hands, for we are brothers dear,
  Of old by tempest rent apart;
The dark designs of cruel Fate
  Shall fail, when heart is joined to heart.
What sound, beneath the stars aflame.
So lovely as a brother's name?

And when our ancient Mother-Land
  Beholds her children side by side,
The dews of joyful tears shall heal
  Her heart's sad wounds, so deep and wide.
What sound, beneath the stars aflame,
So lovely as a brother's name?

We wept together in the past;
  Let us unite in harmony
And blend again our tears, our joys;
  So shall our efforts fruitful be.
What sound, beneath the stars aflame,
So lovely as a brother's name?

Together let us work and strive,
  Together sow, with toil and pain,
The seed that shall, with harvest blest,
  Make bright Armenia's fields again.
What sound, beneath the stars aflame,
So lovely as a brother's name?

Cradle Song

Raphael Patkanian, the most popular of Armenian poets, was born in Southern Russia in 1830. He was the son of poor parents, but both his father and grandfather had been distinguished for their poetic gifts. While at the University of Moscow, he organized a literary club among his Armenian fellow-students, and from the initials of their names formed his own pen-name of Kamar Katiba. Many of his poems were written during the Turco-Russian war, when Russian Armenians cherished high hopes for the deliverance of Turkish Armenia from the Ottoman yoke. Patkanian died in 1892, after 42 years of continuous activity as a teacher, author, & editor.

Nightingale, oh, leave our garden,
  Where soft dews the blossoms steep;
With thy litanies melodious
  Come and sing my son to sleep!
Nay, he sleeps not for thy chanting.
  And his weeping hath not ceased.
Come not, nightingale! My darling
  Does not wish to be a priest.

O thou thievish, clever jackdaw,
  That in coin findest thy joy.
With thy tales of gold and profit
  Come and soothe my wailing boy!
Nay, thy chatter does not lull him,
  And his crying is not stayed.
Come not, jackdaw! for my darling
  Will not choose the merchant's trade.

Wild dove, leave the fields and pastures
  Where thou grievest all day long;
Come and bring my boy sweet slumber
  With thy melancholy song!
Still he weeps. Nay, come not hither,
  Plaintive songster, for I see
That he loves not lamentations,
  And no mourner will he be.

Leave thy chase, brave-hearted falcon!
  Haply he thy song would hear.
And the boy lay hushed, and slumbered,
  With the war-notes in his ear.

The Tears of Araxes

I walk by Mother Arax
  With faltering steps and slow,
And memories of past ages
  Seek in the waters' flow.

But they run dark and turbid,
  And beat upon the shore
In grief and bitter sorrow,
  Lamenting evermore.
"Araxes! with the fishes
  Why dost not dance in glee?
The sea is still far distant.
  Yet thou art sad, like me.

"From thy proud eyes, O Mother,
  Why do the tears downpour?
Why dost thou haste so swiftly
  Past thy familiar shore?

"Make not thy current turbid;
    Flow calm and joyously.
Thy youth is short, fair river;
    Thou soon wilt reach the sea.

"Let sweet rose-hedges brighten
    Thy hospitable shore,
And nightingales among them
    Till morn their music pour.

"Let ever-verdant willows
    Lave in thy waves their feet,
And with their bending branches
    Refresh the noonday heat.

"Let shepherds on thy margin
    Walk singing, without fear;
Let lambs and kids seek freely
    Thy waters cool and clear."

Araxes swelled her current,
    Tossed high her foaming tide,
And in a voice of thunder
    Thus from her depths replied: —

"Rash, thoughtless youth, why com'st thou
    My age-long sleep to break,
And memories of my myriad griefs
    Within my breast to wake?

"When hast thou seen a widow,
    After her true-love died.
From head to foot resplendent
    With ornaments of pride?

"For whom should I adorn me?

Whose eyes shall I delight?
The stranger hordes that tread my banks
    Are hateful in my sight.

"My kindred stream, impetuous Kur,
    Is widowed, like to me,
But bows beneath the tyrant's yoke,
    And wears it slavishly.

"But I, who am Armenian,
    My own Armenians know;
I want no stranger bridegroom;
    A widowed stream I flow.

"Once I, too, moved in splendor,
    Adorned as is a bride
With myriad precious jewels.
    My smiling banks beside.

"My waves were pure and limpid,
    And curled in rippling play;
The morning star within them
    Was mirrored till the day.

"What from that time remaineth?
    All, all has passed away.
Which of my prosperous cities
    Stands near my waves to-day?

"Mount Ararat doth pour me,
    As with a mother's care.
From out her sacred bosom
    Pure water, cool and fair.

"Shall I her holy bounty
    To hated aliens fling?

Shall strangers' fields be watered
    From good Saint Jacob's spring?

"For filthy Turk or Persian
    Shall I my waters pour,
That they may heathen rites perform
    Upon my very shore.

"While my own sons, defenceless,
    Are exiled from their home,
And, faint with thirst and hunger,
    In distant countries roam?

"My own Armenian nation
    Is banished far away;
A godless, barbarous people
    Dwells on my banks to-day.

"Shall I my hospitable shores
    Adorn in festive guise
For them, or gladden with fair looks
    Their wild and evil eyes?

"Still, while my sons are exiled,
    Shall I be sad, as now.
This is my heart's deep utterance,
    My true and holy vow."

No more spake Mother Arax;
    She foamed up mightily.
And, coiling like a serpent.
    Wound sorrowing toward the sea.

The Armenian Girl

Have you seen the bright moon rising

In the heavens? Have you seen
Ruddy apricots that shimmer
    Through the garden's foliage green?

Have you seen the red rose glowing
    Where green leaves about her meet,
And around her, in a bevy,
    Lilies, pinks, and iris sweet?

Lo, beside Armenia's maiden.
    Dark and dim the bright moon is;
Apricots and pinks and iris
    Are not worth a single kiss.

Roses on her cheeks are blooming,
    On her brow a lily fair,
And of innocence the symbol
    Is the smile her sweet lips wear.

From her friend she takes the zither
    With a blush the heart that wins;
Touching it with dainty fingers,
    The lekzinca [1] she begins.

Like a tree her form is slender,
    Swaying with a dreamy grace;
Now she flies with rapid footsteps.
    Now returns with gliding pace.

All the young men's hearts are melted
    When the maiden they behold,
And the old men curse their fortune
    That so early they grew old.

[1] An Oriental dance.

36

The New Generation

When the mother, with sore travail,
  To the world a man-child gives.
Let a sharp sword from his father
  Be the first gift he receives.

As he grows, instead of playthings,
  Toys for childish sport and game,
Let his father give him, rather,
  A good gun, of deadly aim.

When his time is come for schooling,
  Let him to the sword give heed;
Teach him first to wield his weapon;
  After, let him learn to read.

Skill of reading, craft of writing.
  Is a useful thing and good;
But at the examinations
  Ask him first, "Canst thou shed blood?"

Hope ye in no other manner
  Poor Armenia to save.
Ill the beggar's part beseemeth
  Independent men and brave.

Lullaby

Awake, my darling! Open those bright eyes,
dark and deep,
And scatter from thine eyelids the heavy
shades of sleep.
Sweet tales the angels long enough in dreams
have told to thee;

Now I will tell thee of the things thou in the
world shalt see.

Chorus

Awake, and ope thy beauteous eyes, my
child, my little one!
Thy mother sees therein her life, her glory,
and her sun.
Thou shalt grow up, grow tall and strong, as
rises in the air
A stately plane-tree; how I love thy stature
tall and fair!
The heroes of Mount Ararat, their ghosts
shall strengthen thee
With power and might, that thou as brave as
Vartan's self mayst be.
A golden girdle for thy waist my fingers deft
have made,
And from it I have hung a sword, — my own
hands ground the blade.

Within our courtyard stands a steed that,
champing, waits for thee.
Awake, and take thy sword! How long wilt
thou a slumberer be?
Thy nation is in misery; in fetters, lo! they
weep;
Thy brethren are in slavery, my brave one;
wilt thou sleep?

No, soon my son will waken, will mount his
champing steed,
Will wipe away Armenia's tears, and stanch
the hearts that bleed;
Will bid his nation's mourning cease, and
those that weep shall smile.

Ah, my Armenian brethren, wait but a little while!

Lo, my Aghassi has awaked! He girt himself with speed.
And from his sword-belt hung the sword, and mounted on his steed.

To My Nightingale

Why didst thou cease, O nightingale, thy sweet, melodious song,
That to my sad and burning eyes bade floods of teardrops throng?
Dost thou remember, when in spring the dawn was breaking clear,
How often to my heart thou hast recalled my country dear?

Sweet was that memory, as a dream that for a moment's space
Brings joy into a mourner's heart, and brightens his sad face.
The weary world forgotten, to thy voice I bent my ear;
And I was far away, and saw once more my country dear.

I know thou too art longing for that vernal land the while, —
That paradise, afar from which Fate has for us no smile.
Oh, who will give me a bird's wings, that I may sweep and soar,
And cleave the clouds, and hie me to Armenia once more?

If I could breathe her holy and revivifying air,
I know I should be cured at last of all this weight of care.
But when spring passed away it brought thy music to a close,
And took from us thy chanted hymn, with the petals of the rose.

I'll open thy cage door; thou'rt free! Now to Armenia fly!
Dost thou desire the rose, 't is there; there is a cloud- less sky;
There are cool breezes, o'er the fields that softly, sweetly blow;
A sun that shines in splendor, and brooks that murmuring flow.

I too, like thee, am longing for a sunny atmosphere;
The mist and cloud and heavy air have tired my spirit here.
The North wind blows the dust to heaven, the crows with harsh notes sail;
This is the Northern air. and this the Northern nightingale!

O foolish, poor Armenians, what seek ye in the North?
I hate its empty pleasures and its life of little worth.
Give me my country's balmy air. her cloudless sky o'erhead:
Give me my country's pastures green, my country's roses red!

Shall We Be Silent?

Shall we be silent, brothers?
   Shall we be silent still?
Our foe has set against our breasts
   His sword, that thirsts to kill;
His ears are deaf to cries and groans.
   O brothers, make avow!
What shall we do? What is our part?
   Shall we keep silence now?

Our foe has seized our fatherland
   By guile and treachery;
Has blotted out the name of Haig,
   And ruined utterly
The house of Thorkom, to the ground;
   Has reft from us, to boot,
Our crown, our arms, our right of speech —
   And shall we still be mute?

Our foe has seized our guardian swords,
   Our ploughs that tilled the plain,
And from the ploughshare and the sword
   Has welded us a chain.
Alas for us! for we are slaves,
   And fettered hand and foot
With bonds and manacles of iron —
   And shall we still be mute?

Our foeman, holding o'er our heads
   His weapon fierce and strong,
Makes us devour our bitter tears.
   Our protests against wrong.
So many woes are heaped on us,
   To weep our sorrows' sum
We need the broad Euphrates' flood —

And shall we still be dumb?

Our foe, with overweening pride,
   Treads justice under foot,
And drives us from our native soil —
   And shall we still be mute?
Like strangers in our fatherland.
   Pursued o'er plain and hill.
O brothers, where shall we appeal?
   Shall we be silent still?

Not yet content with all the ills
   That he has made us bear,
His insolent and cursed hand
   He stretches forth, to tear
The last bond of our nation's life —
   And, if he have his will,
Complete destruction waits for us;
   Shall we be silent still?

Scorning the glory of our land,
   Our foe, with malice deep.
Invades our church, and makes the wolf
   The shepherd of the sheep.
We have no sacred altars now;
   In valley or on hill
No place of prayer is left to us;
   Shall we be silent still?

If we keep silence, even now,
   When stones have found a voice.
Will not men say that slavery
   Is our desert and choice?
The sons of brave and holy sires,
   Sprung from a sacred root,
We know the deeds our fathers did -

How long shall we be mute?

Mute be the dumb, the paralyzed.
    Those that hold slavery dear!
But we, brave hearts, let us march forth
    To battle, without fear;
And, if the worst befall us,
    Facing the foe like men,
Win back in death our glory,
    And sleep in silence then!

If

If my white hair could once again be black.
And my old strength return to me at need,
And if I could become a valiant youth,
With sword in hand, upon a fiery steed;

I to the field of Avarair would go,
Field where Armenian blood rained down
like dew.
O my loved nation, Thorkom's ancient race!
I would give back your long-lost crown to
you.

To the Armenian maidens I would say:
"Sell now your costly garments beautiful;
Put by adornment, luxury, and pearls;
Our swords are rusty, and their blades are
dull.

"Give us your muslin robes, Armenian
maids,
That we our bleeding wounds may stanch
and stay
Weave bandages for us of your thick hair;
'T is thus you need to show your love to-
day."

Were I a rich man, in whose coffers deep
The gold and silver to great heaps had
grown,
I would not be, as many are. alas!
A patriot in vain words, and words alone.

Not bright champagne, nor Russia's crystal
cross,
But store of balls and powder I would buy;
Against Armenia's foemen I would go
With a great host, freely and fearlessly.

Or if I were a nation's potent king,
I to my army would give strong command
To march with fleet steps toward Armenia,
To help the poor oppressed Armenian land.

But if for one brief day, one little hour,
One moment's space, I were the Lord of all,
What a sharp spear at our blood-thirsty foes
I with strong arm would hurl, and make
them fall!

O guileful Russian! Base and vicious Turk!
O vengeful Persian! O fanatic Greek,
Armenia's age-long rival! On your sons
My two-edged sword should righteous
vengeance wreak!

Praise to the Sultan

Our thanks to you, great Sultan! You have turned
  Armenia to a chaos of hewn stone;
Daily by myriads you have slaughtered us;
  Our thriving hamlets you have overthrown.

Glory and fame unto your Majesty!
  Following the Koran's law, you have not feared
Our holy Bible's pages to defile;
  With filth and mire the cross you have besmeared.

Our gratitude to you, great Padishah!
  Gain from our slaughter has accrued to you;
Your intimate associates you have made
  Circassians foul, and Koords, a thievish crew.

In noisome dungeons, thousands glorify
  Your Sovereign Majesty with loud acclaims.
You leave no blank in all the calendar,
  But fill each space with myriad martyrs' names.

Armenia's happy ruins, glorious King,
  Will ne'er forget you; on our history's page
Your wondrous deeds and your illustrious name
  Shall blazoned be, to live from age to age.

What Shall We Do?

"WHAT shall we do?" Now, shame on those who that weak plaint renew!
He that despairs, in deepest shame his cowardice shall rue.
Armenian brothers, let us ask no more what we shall do!

What does the man do that has chanced to fall into the sea?
What does he do that has no bread, and starves in poverty?
What does he do that has been seized and bound in slavery?

He that is drowning in the sea struggles with all his might;
The hungry man wears out his neighbors threshold day and night;
He that is in captivity seeks ever means of flight.

O rich man, for what purpose hast thou filled thy chests with gold?
O youth, for what hast thou reserved thy strength, thy courage bold?
O patriot, wherefore hast thou loved thy country from of old?
Let us no more the plaint renew,
"Armenians, say, what shall we do?"

The Sad-Faced Moon

(From "The Death of Vartan.")

Moon, fair moon, how long wilt thou appear
  So pale, so mournful, in the heavens'
height?
Have the dark storm-clouds filled thee with
alarm.
  Or fiery lightnings, flashing through the
night?

There is none like to thee among the stars;
  The only beauty of the heavens thou art.
Hast thou grown pale with envy? Nay, O
moon,
  Thou hast some other secret in thy heart.

Why is thy countenance thus changed and
sad?
  Speak to me freely! On the darkest day.
If we but find a sympathizing friend
  It is said that half our grief will pass away.

The mourner is the mourner's comforter.
  Where wilt thou find a sadder man than I,
Forsaken and in sorrow, and. like thee.
  Hiding a secret, without word or cry?

I pass my days in grief, gay among men.
  Weeping in solitude; my salt tears flow,
My sad sighs sound forever, without rest;
  I have no sympathizer in my woe.

Yet every living creature has a friend;
  Shall I alone lack love and friendship? Nay,

Open thy heart to me! If thou art sad,
  My sympathy will charm thy grief away.

(*The moon speaks.*)

Hearken! One night innumerable stars
  Filled the blue sky. Among them, like a
bride.
I glided softly, with my bright face veiled.
  I passed o'er Pontus, bathing in its tide;

I touched the summits of the Caucasus;
  I saw in Lake Sevan my mirrored face;
I came to great Lake Van, of fishes full,
  And cooled me in its waves a little space.

O'er many mountains, many fields I passed.
  Shedding my light; o'er all reigned silence
deep;
Amid his cattle in the quiet field
  The weary farmer lay in peaceful sleep.

Ah, fair Armenia on that night was blest!
  The stars of heaven made her more glori-
ous still;
And I, slow passing o'er her through the
skies,
  Gazed on that land, and could not gaze my
fill.

In one short month, my circuit I renewed.
  O'er cities, mountains, lakes, I passed in
haste,
Longing to visit the Armenian land.
  Night had again her fruitful fields em-
braced;

But oh! where were the bounteous harvests now?
  Where was the tireless tiller of the soil?
Where was his little thick-necked buffalo?
  Where were the gardens, product of his toil?

Dark smoke had covered the Armenian sky;
  Cities and hamlets, burning, crashed and fell;
Fierce tongues of flame reached even to the clouds;
  To see Armenia was to gaze on hell!

Armenia, garden wet with heavenly dew!
  Whence came this mighty woe, at whose behest?
Did jealousy possess his evil heart?
  Had in his soul a serpent made its nest?

Yes, it was age-long jealousy and hate,
  That, smouldering deep, consume man's heart away,
Until at last, with fierce and thundering sound,
  The hidden fires break forth, to scorch and slay;

Like to a mountain, still and calm without.
  On which the smooth snow all unmelted sleeps;
Suddenly, lightnings from its breast are born,
  And o'er whole cities fiery ruin sweeps.

O fair Armenian land! Armenian race!
  O happy places, ruined now and void!

Hamlets and cornfields, cloisters, teeming towns!
  Where are you? Why were you so soon destroyed?

- - - - - - - -

The moon was silent. And the dark clouds came
  And hid the sky; she passed behind a cloud;
And I was left alone and sorrowful,
  Musing with folded arms and forehead bowed.

And ever since that time, when evening comes,
  I wait the pale moon's rising, calm and slow;
And as I gaze upon her mournful face,
  I think upon my nation and its woe.

Complaint to Europe

My hands, my feet, the chain of slavery ties,
Yet Europe says, "Why do you not arise?
Justice nor freedom shall your portion he;
Bear to the end the doom of slavery!"

Six centuries, drop by drop, the tyrant drains
The last remaining life-blood from our veins;
Yet Europe says, "No strength, no power have they,"
And turns from us her scornful face away.

A needle is not left to us to-day,
And yet, "You ought to draw the sword!"
they say.

43

To powder and to shot could we give heed,
While we sought bread our starving ones to
feed?

Have you forgotten, Europe, how the dart
Of the fierce Persian pointed at your henrt,
Until, on that dread field of Avarair,
Armenian blood quenched his fanatic fire? [1]

Have you forgot the fell and crushing blow
Prepared for you by Islam long ago?
We would not see your desolation then,
Burning of cities, massacre of men.

Two hundred years Armenia, bathed in
blood,
Withstood that great invasion's mighty flood.
Europe was safe, our living wall behind,
Until the enemy's huge strength declined.

Have you forgotten, Europe, how of yore
Your heroes in the desert hungered sore?
What then could strength or force of arms
avail,
Had we not fed your hosts, with famine pale?
[2]

Ungrateful Europe, heed our woes, we pray:
Remember poor Armenia to-day!

[1] Geographically, Armenia is the bridge be-
tween Europe and Asia. In the early centuries the
Armenians acted the part of Horatius and "kept
the bridge," defending the gate of Europe against
the uncivilized hordes of Asia, — first against the
Persian fire-worshippers, whose advance toward
Europe the Armenians checked at the battle of
Avarair in A. D. 451, and later against successive
invasions of the Mohammedans.

[2] The Armenians acted as guides to the Cru-
saders in Asia; and when they were about to raise
the siege of Antioch for want of food, the Arme-
nians of Cilicia supplied them with
provisions and enabled them to take the city.

Song of the Van Mother

I will not rock you, little boy, that sleep your
soul may bind;
Your brothers have arisen; you only stay
behind.
Awake from sleep, my darling! From the
West hath shone the sun.
Awake! The happy fortune of Armenia has
begun.

Lo, it is fallen, dashed to bits, the Sultan's
golden throne!
From under it the liberty of many lands hath
shone.
Now he who speedily shall rise shall find his
liberty:
Will my fair son alone remain fast bound in
slavery?

We have implored the Sultan with mourning
and with cries;
We washed his hands, we washed his feet,
with salt tears from our eyes.
He would not heed our piteous prayers, our
sad, beseeching words;
Now let us see if he will heed the clashing of
our swords!

44

My darling, let me from thine arms unbind
the swaddling band,
And lay a sword of steel within that weak
and tender hand!
Go to the bloody battlefield, O slave, and
come back freed!
O Lord, our God, wilt thou one day unto our
prayer give heed?

Easter Song

*This Easter song is sung by the children. In
Turkey and Russia the last verse is forbidden.*

Underneath the south wind's breathing,
　From the fields the snow has fled;
All the children are rejoicing —
　Christ is risen from the dead!

Brooks with happy voices murmur.
　Boughs are budding overhead,
All the air is full of bird-songs —
　Christ is risen from the dead!

Boys and girls wear festal raiment,
　As in May the rose so red;
Hatred from man's heart is banished
　Christ is risen from the dead!

Christ is risen, all Nature tells ns;
　When, ah! when shall it be said
Of thee also, O my country!
　Thou art risen from the dead?

The Virgin's Tears

*Leo Alishan, born at Erzerum, in the heart of
Armenia, early in the last century, was a
Roman Catholic Armenian, a monk of the
Mechitarist Convent at Venice, and a distin-
guished antiquarian, scientist, linguist, and
historian, as well as a poet. He is the author
of many important works in these different
fields, and translated into Armenian a num-
ber of poems by Longfellow and other Amer-
ican writers. Alishan was loved and revered
by his countrymen, not only for his erudition
and patriotism, but for his gentle and unas-
suming disposition.*

Forth welling from the breast of sapphire
lakes,
　Oh, tell my jocund heart why from their
shore
Of emerald do those pairs of wandering
pearls
　Like rain upon the rosy plains downpour?

Less pure, less tender, are the twilight dews,
　At eve descending on the crimson rose
And on the lily's petals, fine and frail,
　Than those twin drops in which thy sorrow
flows.

Speak, why do founts of shining tears de-
scend,
　Mary, from thy love-dropping virgin eyes
To thy cheek's edge, and there hang tremu-
lous.
　As the stars twinkle in the evening skies?

45

As the heart-piercing pupil of the eye,
   So sensitive each tear-drop seems to be;
Like the unwinking pupil of the eye,
   Charming my soul, the bright drops look
at me.

The heart throbs hard, the gazer holds his
breath.
   Ah, now I know the truth! Oh, woe is me!
For me those tears have risen to thine eyes,
   To heal my spirit's wounds eternally.

But still of my unconsecrated heart
   Distrustful, they half-fallen linger there,
And do not dare to drop and moisten me.
   No, Mary! No, O Virgin Mother fair!

I am a land uncultured, rough and wild;
   But, underneath those tender tears of
thine,
Let rose and saffron bloom there! With thy
love
   Water and cheer this sorrowing heart of
mine!

Easter Song

Father of light, we praise thee!
   Thy Son is risen again.
Spirit of love, we praise thee!
   He shares thy glorious reign.

Good tidings, Virgin Princess!
   Thy Son is risen this morn.
Good tidings to all mortals.
   The born and the unborn!

Good news to you, bright Heavens!
   For Christ, who dwelt in you,
Is risen; good tidings, lowly Earth!
   Thy Saviour lives anew.

Good news to you, all worlds and orbs
   That circle overhead!
Good news! Your great Establisher
   Is risen from the dead!

Good news, ye light and darkness!
   A new sun rises high.
Good news to you, all creatures!
   Christ lives; you shall not die.

Good news to you, ye dead folk I
   For you shall be set free.
Good tidings to all beings
   That are, or are to be!

The Exiles

Alas, ye poor Armenians!
   In undeserved distress
Ye wander forth to slavery,
   In want and wretchedness.

A myriad woes ye suffered,
   Nor left your own dear home;
But now ye leave your fathers' graves,
   In distant lands to roam.

These waters sweet, these sniiUng fields.
   Where cities fair are set,
To strangers ye abandon them,
   But how can ye forget?

Nay, while you live, remember;
  Be to your country true:
Your children and descendants.
  Bid them remember too.

The holy name of Ararat
  And many a sacred fane.
Till the last judgment wakes the world,
  Shall in their hearts remain.

Alas for thee, my country!
  Alas for thee, for us!
I would that death had sealed mine eyes
  Ere I beheld thee thus!

Moon in the Armenian Cemetery

O moon, fair lamp divinely lit!
  God set you in the sky
To lead night's hosts, for darkness blind
  And for my heart an eye.

When o'er my head you swing, your lamp
  A glittering chain doth hold;
Your string of heavenly silver is,
  Your wick of burning gold;

And, as a diamond flashes light,
  You shed your rays abroad.
How bright you were, that second night,
  Fresh from the hand of God!

How bright you were when first was heard
  The heavenly nightingale!
The wind, that seemed like you alive,
  Played soft from vale to vale;

With that calm breeze, the limpid brook
  Plashed in an undertone;
There was no human ear to hear.
  The angels heard alone.

The angels swung you in their hands,
  And silently and slow
You traversed heaven's cloudless arch,
  And sank the waves below,

What time the sun with feet of fire
  Was soon to mount the blue,
While o'er the silent world were spread
  Twilight and hoary dew.

Stay, stay, O sun! awhile delay;
  Rise not in the blue sky,
But let the little moon still walk
  The cloudless realm on high!

Stay, little moon! Oh, linger yet
  Upon the heights and hills;
Pass slowly, calmly, where your light
  The sleeping valleys fills!

For I have words to utter yet.
  To you I would complain.
Oh, many are my bitter griefs,
  My heart is cleft in twain.

Bright moon, haste not away because
  You hear a mourner's cry!
As comforter of broken hearts
  You shine there in the sky.

You come to Eden's land, but not

As on that far first night,
When man was happy, knowing naught
Save life and love's delight.

Then your white radiance was warm
To waves and flowerets fair,
And wheresoe'er your soft light fell,
Immortal life bloomed there.

Turn and look down on me, O moon!
Craze at our mountains' foot,
And see the ruined temples there,
And tombs so sad and mute, —

Tombs of Armenians who long since
From earth have passed away.
There sleep the ashes of our sires,
In darkness and decay.

Armenians they, the earliest born
Of all the human race.
Who had their home within the land
Once Adam's dwelling-place.

(*Here follows a long list of Armenian kings.*)

But you are setting fast, O moon!
Your lustre fades away,
And like a silver plate you sink
In cloud-banks dense and gray.

Stay yet a moment's space, O moon,
Stay for the love of me!
There in the valley is one stone
Unknown to history.

Go, let your last light linger there.
And lift it out of gloom,
For that obscure and nameless stone
Will mark the poet's tomb!

The Lily of Shavarshan

This is an extract from a long poem in the classical Armenian, describing the conversion to Christianity by the Apostle Thaddeus, in the first century A. D., of Santoukhd, the daughter of the Armenian King Sanadroog. Both the princess and the apostle were put to death by the king. According to Armenian tradition, Santoukhd was the earliest Christian martyr among women.

Armenian maidens, come and view
In Shavarshan a lily new!

The radiant type of maidenhood,
Crown of Armenia's pride!
From the fair brow beneath her veil
The wind-stirred curls float wide.
With little steps, like turtle dove,
She walks the dew-bright plain;
Her lips drop honey, and her eyes
Effulgent glances rain.

The beauty of Armenia,
A sun-like mirror clear.
Our Northern star is bright Santoukhd,
The king's fair daughter dear.
She has come forth, the graceful bride
On whom the East and West
Desire to look, while fires of love

Consume the gazer's breast.

Less fair the bright and morning star,
'Mid cloudlets small and fine;
Less fair the fruit whose rosy tints
'Mid apple leaves outshine;
Araxes' hyacinthine flower
That chains of dew doth wear.
All are less beautiful than she,
With gracious mien and air.

At sight of her, the snowy peaks
Melt and are flushed with rose;
Trees, flowers bud forth; the nightingales
All sing where'er she goes.
The bell-flowers open myriad eyes
When she comes through the bowers;
Beneath her breath, the vales and hills
Alike are clad in flowers.

Before her have been bent to earth
Foreheads with diadems;
The valley has become a hill
Of scattered gold and gems.
Where passes by with humble grace
Armenia's virgin sweet,
Fine sands of pearls come longingly
To spread beneath her feet.

Full many a monarch's valiant son
Has left his palace home
In Persia or Albania,
In India or in Rome.
Admiringly they gaze on her,
Exclaiming, "Happy he
Who wins the fair Armenian maid

His bride beloved to be!"

But palace worthy of Santoukhd
The earth can nowhere show,
And for the arches of her brows
This world is all too low.
The Sky says, "Let her on my throne
Reign queen o'er every land."
The Ocean says, "My purple waves
Shall bow to her command."

There is one greater than the earth,
More wide than sea-waves run,
Higher and vaster than the heavens,
And brighter than the sun.
There is a formidable King
Whose power no bound has known;
The royal maid Santoukhd shall be
For him, and him alone.
Her halls of light are all prepared,
And for a footstool meet
The azure sky adorned with stars
Awaits her dove-like feet.

- - - - - -

The sharp sword glitters in the air,
And swift the red blood flows;
Santoukhd, who was a lily fair,
Falls to the earth, a rose.
The sword flashed once, and aspects three
Were in Santoukhd descried;
Her heart dropped blood, and roses red
Sprang up on every side;
Her eyes were violet chalices,
Sweet e'en while they expire;
Her face, like lilies half unclosed,
But on her lips what fire!

49

The heaven and earth shine white and red;
  Come forth and gather, maids,
The rose and lily joined in one,
  This peerless flower that fades!
Lay in the tomb that youthful corpse,
  With Thaddeus, good and brave.
Sweet maiden of Armenia,
  Her sweet soil be thy grave!
Armenian maids, a lily new
  Is brought to Shavarshan for you!

The Nightingale of Avarair

Whence dost thou come, O moon, so calmly and softly,
  Spreading o'er mountain, valley, and plain thy light,
And over me the Patriarch, wandering sadly.
  With wandering thoughts, in Avarair to-night?

Mere where our matchless, brave Armenian fathers
  Fell as giants, as angels to rise anew,
Com'st thou to spread o'er the bones of the saints a cover
  Of golden thread, from thy cloud of snowy hue?

Or dost thou think, though thy brow be bright already,
  Adornment of heroes' blood would become it well?
Or dost thou still, in silence and secret, wonder

To think how the great and terrible Vartan fell,

Giving his enemies' lives to the shades of darkness.
  And giving his spirit into the hands of God?
And thou, O River Deghmoud, thou flowest lamenting
  Amid thy reeds, sad river bestained with blood.

And thou, O wind from Manguran's upland blowing,
  Or Ararat's sacred summit, gray-haired and hoar,
Thou, too, like me, uncertain and trembling movest,
  On faint wings passing the mountains and valleys o'er.

From forest to forest, from leaf to leaf, lamenting,
  Thou comest upon the plains, in pale moonshine,
To carry unto Armenian hearts the echo
  Of the last sighs of this worn heart of mine.

Nightingale, voice of the night, little soul of the roses,
  Friend of all mournful hearts that with sorrow are sighing!
Sing, little nightingale, sing me a song from that hillock,

Sing with my soul of Armenia's heroes undying!

Thy voice in the cloister of Thaddeus reached me and thrilled me;
My heart, that was close to the cross, in a reverie grave.
Suddenly bounded and throbbed; from the cross I hastened to seek thee —
Came forth and found thee here, on the field of Vartan the brave.

Nightingale, this is the tale that of thee our fathers have told us:
That Avarair's nightingale, singing so sweetly at daylight's dim close.
Is not a bird, but a soul, — it is Eghiche's [1] sweet-voiced spirit,
That sees the image of Vartan for aye in the red-blooming rose.

In winter he walks alone, and mourns in the midst of the desert;
In spring comes to Avarair, to the bush with roses aflame.
To sing and to call aloud, with Eghiche's voice, upon Vartan,
To see whether Vartan perchance will answer when called by his name.

If like the voice of a nightingale faint and weary,
Sons of Togarmah, my voice shall reach your ears,—
Sons of the great, whose valiant and virtuous fathers

Filled plains, books, and the heavens, in former years, —

If one small drop of blood from Armenia's fountain.
The fount of Bahlav, flow into your bosoms' sea, —
If you would that your country's glories for you be written,
Come forth to Ardaz with your Patriarch, come with me!

[1] An Armenian historian of the fifth century, a contemporary of Vartan. In his history of the Persian invasion he compares Vartan drenched in his blood, to the red rose.

A Song of Fatherland

We are the sons of valiant men, Armenians great and free;
Our grandsires were descended from a hero-ancestry;
Our fathers brave on Ararat were strong to draw the bow;
Our Haig, the son of Japhet, laid haughty Nimrod low.
From mountains high, from giants proud, this race of warriors starts.
Then, ardent brothers, let us possess Armenian hearts!

Lift up your eyes unto the heights that pierce the heavens vast,
The land that was the cradle of all nations in the past.

God on free Ararat abides, and raises in the air.
To give us hope, a temple built of seven colors fair.
The hearts of the Armenians with courage to inspire.
He spans the heavens with a wide and wondrous arch of fire.

No nation can survive unless it glows with patriot flame;
No son of the Armenian race is worthy of his name
Unless to all the virtues of his fathers he aspires.
Then let ns, brothers, emulous of our exalted sires,

Now gird ourselves for usefulness, to serve in word and deed.
To the vain words of foreigners no more let us give heed,
But let the spirit bright of Haig sway all our inward powers.
Then, brothers, ardent brothers, Armenian souls be ours!

Brothers, let hand to hand be pressed, and heart to heart, in love,
And toward one common object together let us move;
And let the touch of fiery lips unite our minds in one,
While in all hearts a common pulse shall beat in unison!

Let us from tombs and monuments decipher and unfold
The glorious deeds achieved by our immortal sires of old,
To show to all the nations round our ancestors of fame.
And show our ancestors, in us, sons worthy of their name!

To the arena, patriots, go forth and cry, "Behold,
We are the children of those great Armenians of old!
Through us a new Armenia in splendor shall arise.
And cast away the sombre veil that hid her from men's eyes,
Armenia, sit no longer mute and hidden in the shade!
Through us among the nations shall thy name be glorious made.
Loyal until our deaths, for thee we'll strive with heart and hand."
Then, brothers, ardent brothers, long live our native land!

Weep Not

Why art thou troubled, wandering heart?
  Why dost thou sigh with pain?
From whom do all thy sufferings come?
  Of whom dost thou complain?

Is there no cure for wounds, no friend
  To lend a pitying ear?
Why art thou troubled, wandering heart?

Weep not! See Jesus near!

Sorrow and hardship are for all,
   Though differing forms they wear.
The path he gave us teems with thorns.
   The feet must suffer there.

What life, though but a day's brief span,
   Is free from pain and woe?
'T is not for mortals born in grief
   To live at ease below.

Not for the transient joys of earth
   Thy heart to thee was given,
But for an instrument of grief,
   To raise thy life toward heaven.

If joys be few, if pains abound,
   If balms bring slow relief,
If wounds be sore and nature weak,
   Thy earthly life is brief

This is the vale of death and pain,
   Ordained for ancient sin;
Except through anguish, Eden's gate
   No soul shall enter in.

Justice ordained it; mercy then
   Made it more light to bear.
Unasked by thee, Christ sweetened it,
   His love infusing there.

From heaven's height he hastened down,
   Pitying thy trouble sore;
With thee a servant he became.
   Himself thy wounds he bore.

He filled his cup celestial
   Full of thy tears and pain,
And tremblingly, yet freely.
   He dared the dre<is to drain.

Remembering this, wilt thou not drink
   Thy cup of tears and care?
'T is proffered by thy Saviour's hand,
   His love is mingled there.

He feels and pities all thy woes,
   He wipes away each tear;
Love he distils into thy griefs;
   Weep not, for he is near!

Miscellaneous

The Christ-Child

By Saint Gregory of Narek (Born 951; Died 1011).

The lips of the Christ-child are like to twin leaves;
They let roses fall when he smiles tenderly.
The tears of the Christ-child are pearls when he grieves;
The eyes of the Christ-child are deep as the sea.
Like pomegranate grains are the dimples he hath,
And clustering lilies spring up in his path.

Hymn

By Nerses the Graceful (Born 1102; Died 1172).

O day-Spring, Sun of righteousness, shine
forth with light for me!
Treasure of mercy, let my soul thy hidden
riches see!

Thou before whom the thoughts of men lie
open in thy sight,
Unto my soul, now dark and dim, grant
thoughts that shine with light.

O Father, Son, and Holy Ghost, Almighty
One in Three,
Care-taker of all creatures, have pity upon
me!

Awake, O Lord, awake to help, with grace
and power divine;
Awaken those who slumber now, like heav-
en's host to shine!

O Lord and Saviour, life-giver, unto the dead
give life.
And raise up those that have grown weak
and stumbled in the strife.

O skilful Pilot! Lamp of light, that burnest
bright and clear!
Strength and assurance grant to me. now hid
away in fear!

O thou that makest old things new, renew
me and adorn;

Rejoice me with salvation. Lord, for which I
inly mourn.

Giver of good, unto my sins be thy for-
giveness given!
Lead thy disciples, heavenly King, unto the
flocks of heaven!

Defeat the evil husbandman that soweth tares
and weeds;
Wither and kill in me the fruits of all his evil
seeds!

O Lord, grant water to my eyes, that they
may shed warm tears
To cleanse and wash away the sin that in my
soul appears!

On me now hid in shadow deep, shine forth,
O glory bright!
Sweet juice, quench thou my soul's keen
thirst! Show me the path of light!

Jesus, whose name is love, with love crush
thou my stony heart;
Bedew my spirit with thy blood, and bid my
griefs depart!

O thou that even in fancy art so sweet. Lord
Jesus Christ,
Grant that with thy reality my soul may be
sufficed!

When thou shalt come again to earth, and all
thy glory see,

Upon that dread and awful day, O Christ, remember me!

Thou that redeemest men from sin, O Saviour, I implore,
Redeem him who now praises thee, to praise thee evermore!

Love Song

By Saïat Nova (Born 1712; Died 1795).

I sigh not, while thou art my soul! Fair one, thou art to me
A golden cup, with water filled of immortality.
I sit me down, that over me may fall thy shadow, sweet;
Thou art a gold-embroidered tent to shield me from the heat.
First hear my fault, and, if thou wilt, then slay this erring man;
Thou hast all power; to me thou art the Sultan and the Khan.

Thy waist is like a cypress-tree, sugar thy tongue, in sooth;
Thy lip is candy, and thy skin like Frankish satin smooth.
Thy teeth are pearls and diamonds, the gates of dulcet tones;
Thine eyes are gold-enamelled cups adorned with precious stones.
Thou art a rare and priceless gem, most wonderful to see;

A ruby rich of Mt. Bedakhsh, my love, thou art to me.

How can I bear this misery, unless my heart were stone?
My tears are blood because of thee, my reason is o'erthrown.
A young vine in the garden fresh thou art to me. my fair.
Enshrined in greenness, and set round with roses everywhere.
I, like the love-lorn nightingale, would hover over thee.
A landscape of delight and love, my queen, thou art to me!

Lo, I am drunken with thy love! I wake, but my heart sleeps.
The world is sated with the world; my heart its hunger keeps.
What shall I praise thee by, when naught is left on earth save thee?
Thou art a deer, a Pegasus sprung from the fiery sea!

Speak but one word, to say thou art Saïat Nova's [1] love.
And then what matters aught to me, in earth or heaven above?
Thy rays have filled the world; thou art a shield that fronts the sun.
Thou dost exhale the perfume sweet of clove and cinnamon.
Of violet, rose, and marjoram; to me, with love grown pale,

Thou art a red flower of the field, a lily of the vale!

[1] An Armenian minstrel often weaves his name into the last stanza of his song, in order that he may be known as its composer. The same peculiarity appears in the next poem.

A Good Comrade

A good comrade, beautiful and virtuous,
  Lights man's face up, like a bright sun-ray.
When a man has with him a true comrade,
  Dark night passes like a sunny day.

Sacrifice is nothing; a kind comrade
  Is the spirit's lamp of light and fire.
A good friend, a true, God-fearing comrade,
  Leads man ever upward, high and higher.

When our enemies attack us fiercely,
  A brave comrade is a sword in fight.
Whoso has a true friend, singer Djivan,
  Never shall one hair of his turn white.

The Youth and the Streamlet

Down from yon distant mountain
  The streamlet finds its way,
And through the quiet village
  It flows in eddying play.

A dark youth left his doorway,
  And sought the water-side,
And, laving there his hands and brow.
  "O streamlet sweet!" he cried,

"Say, from what mountain com'st thou?
  "From yonder mountain cold
Where snow on snow lies sleeping,
  The new snow on the old."

"Unto what river, tell me,
  Fair streamlet, dost thou flow?"
"I flow unto that river
  Where clustering; violets grow."

"Sweet streamlet, to what vineyard,
  Say, dost thou take thy way?"
"The vineyard where the vine-dresser
  Is at his work to-day."

"What plant there wilt thou water?"
  "The plant upon whose roots
The lambs feed, where the wind-flower blooms,
  And orchards bear sweet fruits."

"What garden wilt thou visit,
  O water cool and fleet?"
"The garden where the nightingale
  Sings tenderly and sweet."

"Into what fountain flow'st thou?"
  "The fountain to whose brink
Thy love comes down at morn and eve,
  And bends her face to drink.

"There shall I meet the maiden
  Who is to be thy bride.
And kiss her chin, and with her love
  My soul be satisfied."

The Lake of Van

By "Raffi" (Melik Hagopian).

Speak, O lake! why are thy waters silent?
  Wilt thou not lament with luckless me?
Move, ye zephyrs, move the rippling wave-
lets!
  With this lake my tears shall mingled be.

Tell me, lake, — for thou hast been a witness
  Of our history from the earliest day, —
Shall Armenia, that was once a garden.
  Always be a thorny desert gray?

Shall our hapless fatherland forever
  By a foreign master be down-trod?
Are the Armenians and their sons unworthy,
  Judged before the righteous throne of God?

Is a glad day coming, when a banner
  Shall on Ararat its folds expand.
And from every side Armenian pilgrims
  Hasten to their beauteous fatherland?

Thou and I

Would I were the lake, so blue and calm,
  And thou, fair maiden, with reluctant pride,
Wouldst see thy picture, delicate and faint,
  Thy sacred image, in my depths abide.

Or would that on the shore a willow grew.
  And thou mightst lean on it, and the frail
tree
Might let thee fall into the lake, and there

Sway with its waters everlastingly!

I would I were the forest, dark and vast,
  And that thou there mightst come to muse
alone,
And, ere I knew it, I might overhear
  What thy lips murmur in an undertone.

Or would that thou mightst sit beneath a
tree,
  Singing a pure, sweet song; and leaf and
bough.
With admiration trembling, would descend
  And form a coronal to wreathe thy brow.

I would I were the face of the dark sky.
  That so from heaven I might shake down
on thee
A multitude of stars, as 't were my tears;
  Ah, do not tread upon them scornfully!

Would I the writer were, and thou the
theme!
  Would thou affection wert, and I the heart!
I the bouquet, and thou its silken string;
  When thou art loosed, the flowers will fall
apart.

Oh, would I were a lover of sweet song,
  And thou my lyre, angel for whom I pine!
And that thy chords beneath my unskilled
hands
  Might vibrate till thy heart responds to
mine!

To My Sweetheart

When my glance wanders to the far-off
deeps,
    Beauteous and infinite, of the blue skies,
Behind transparent cloud-veils, fold on fold, -
    Then I recall your melancholy eyes.

When from the delicate light clouds descends
    The fresh, cool dew of morning, and ap-
pears,
Like a bright veil, upon the red-cheeked rose,
    I think of your deep eyes, those lakes of
tears.

When the fair rainbow with its splendid hues
    Has in its arch the height of heaven em-
braced,
I wish I were its owner and its lord.
    That I might gird with it your dainty waist.

When the stars, bright and dazzling, glow
like fire,
    And with their gems the midnight heaven
deck.
My heart's pangs are more numerous than
they,
    That they should not adorn your breast
and neck.

My tender love, my sweetheart fair to see,
    Now parted from my arms forevermore,
She is my hapless fair Armenia,
    Whom I have loved, and ever shall adore.

The Chraghan Palace

By T. Terzyan

Have you ever seen that wondrous building,
    Whose white shadows in the blue wave
sleep?
There Carrara sent vast mounds of marble,
    And Propontis, beauty of the deep.

From the tombs of centuries awaking,
    Souls of every clime and every land
Have poured forth their rarest gifts and
treasures
    Where those shining halls in glory stand.

Ships that pass before that stately palace,
    Gliding by with open sails agleam,
In its shadow pause and gaze, astonished,
    Thinking it some Oriental dream.

New its form, more wondrous than the
Gothic,
    Than the Doric or Ionic fair;
At command of an Armenian genius [1]
    Did the master builder rear it there.

By the windows, rich with twisted scroll-work,
    Rising upward, marble columns shine,
And the sunbeams lose their way there, wan-
dering
    Where a myriad ornaments entwine.

An immortal smile, its bright reflection
    In the water of the blue sea lies,
And it shames Granada's famed Alhambra,

O'er whose beauty wondering bend the
skies.

Oft at midnight, in the pale, faint starlight,
    When its airy outline, clear and fair,
On the far horizon is depicted,
    With its trees and groves around it there,

You can fancy that those stones grow living,
    And, amid the darkness of the night,
Change to lovely songs, to which the spirit,
    Dreaming, listens with a vague delight.

Have you ever seen that wondrous building
    Whose white shadows in the blue wave
sleep?
There Marmora sent vast mounds of marble,
    And Propontis, beauty of the deep.

It is not a mass of earthly matter,
    Not a work from clay or marble wrought;
From the mind of an Armenian genius
    Stands embodied there a noble thought.

[1] The late Hagop Bey Balian.

The Wandering Armenian to the
Swallow

By C. A. Totochian

O swallow, gentle swallow,
    Thou lovely bird of spring!
Say, whither art thou flying
    So swift on gleaming wing?

Fly to my birthplace, Ashdarag,
    The spot I love the best;
Beneath my father's roof-tree,
    O swallow, build thy nest.

There dwells afar my father,
    A mournful man and gray,
Who for his only son's return
    Waits vainly, day by day.

If thou shouldst chance to see him.
    Greet him with love from me;
Bid him sit down and mourn with tears
    His son's sad destiny.

In poverty and loneliness,
    Tell him, my days are passed:
My life is only half a life,
    My tears are falling fast.

To me, amid bright daylight,
    The sun is dark at noon;
To my wet eyes at midnight
    Sleep comes not, late or soon.

Tell him that, like a beauteous flower
    Smit by a cruel doom,
Uprooted from my native soil,
    I wither ere my bloom.

Fly on swift wing, dear swallow,
    Across the quickening earth,
And seek in fair Armenia
    The village of my birth!

59

Song of Revolution

If on the ocean tempest-tossed
My shattered bark be wrecked and lost,
Amid the wild and raging sea
All hope shall not depart from me.

With all my power, with steadfast will,
I'll wage a swimmer's battle still,
And, cleaving mighty waves that roar,
I'll urge my pathway toward the shore.

And if in this unequal strife
My powers succumb, and fails my life, —
If whirling waves that foam and hiss
Shall whelm me in the deep abyss, —

One great, sweet thought shall serve to fill
My heart with consolation still:
That hero-like my spirit passed,
Contending bravely to the last.

The Lament of Mother Armenia

In alien lands they roam, my children dear;
Where shall I make appeal, with none to hear?

Where shall I find them? Far away from me
My sons serve others, thralls in slavery.

Chorus.

Oh, come, my children, back to me!
Come home, your motherland to see!

Ages have passed, no news of them I hear;
Dead, dead are they, my sons that knew not fear.
I weep, the blood is frozen in my veins;
No one will cure my sorrows and my pains.

My blood is failing and my heart outworn,
My face forever mournful and forlorn;
To my dark grave with grief I shall descend,
Longing to see my children to the end.

O wandering shepherd, you whose mournful song
Rings through the valleys as you pass along!
Come, let us both, with many a bitter tear,
Weep for the sad death of our children dear!

Crane of the fatherland, fly far away,
Fly out of sight, beyond the setting day;
My last sad greetings to my children bear,
For my life's hope has died into despair!

The Son of Dalvorig

By Mihran Damadian

Brave son of Dalvorig, Dalvorig's son am I;
  Son am I of the mountain, son am I of the rock.
Not like the timid dwellers in city walls am I;
  I am the remnant of the old, the brave Armenian stock.
The brave son of Dalvorig, Dalvorig's son am I,
  And in the presence of the Turk I do not cringe or bow;

60

The free son of the rocky hills, the rugged heights, am I;

My eyes have never looked upon the plough-haft or the plough.

Chorus

Ho, my Armenian brothers. Dalvorig's son am I;
Oh, come to me, come hither, for the love of liberty!

When on the world I ope'd my eyes I saw our mountains high,
Our rocks and cliffs; our mountains, our rocks and cliffs were free.
Until I close my eyes upon the darkness when I die,
Ne'er shall the feet of foreigners tread here triumphantly.
My mother gave me birth in a narrow, rocky gorge,
The strong branch of a walnut tree my cradle-bed became;
So plain and simple was my birth, so plainly I was reared.
My portion in this earthly life is conflict, fire, and flame.

My feet are bare, my chest exposed; but what for that care I,
If only my young sister may grow up free like me?
To me the sunshine and the cold and mist are all the same,
So long as here the Turk and Koord have no authority.

My life is hard, my life is rough; I never have been used
To dwell at ease in luxury and feed on dainty fare.
I do not live in palace halls, my dwelling is the rock,
The tempest and the earthquake are my companions there.

Let other men inhabit the valleys and the plains.
And with the base and ruthless Turk on terms of friendship be;
I will remain unvanquished forever and a day,
Even if twenty squadrons should come to vanquish me.

Instead of tender wheaten bread, the millet is my food;
I forge the red-hot iron day and night, incessantly;
I make cross-irons for griddles, and spades to till the soil;
Men look upon my lot in life as hard, but I am free.

High genius and the homage of the mind are not for me;
Enough for me it is to have my dagger and my sword;
Enough for me it is to know that while the mountains stand
No foreigner shall ever be my master and my lord.

61

My arms my only playthings are; comfort I hate, and ease;

A quiet and a placid life upon me soon would pall.
I love the chase, I love the fight, I love the fight's reward,

And I am ever ready when comes the signal call.

When the alarm is given, then fearless I start forth;

The mountains of Sassoun breathe a sigh and cry aloud —
They cry aloud, and over them there spreads a crimson stain;

The red stain on the mountains, it is their heroes' blood.

The hero's heart, the hero's hand! What does the hero care

Although a thousand wounds and one should pierce him, blow on blow?
For every blow men deal him, a thousand he returns;

He strews the earth with corpses, a banquet for the crow.

I leap upon the mountains as leaps the mountain deer;

The thunder of my angry voice the lion's roar is like;
I foam as foams the ocean, fierce beating on the shore;

And when I smite the foeman, as a thunderbolt I strike.

The stormy field of battle is my portion in this life;

There either the red sunset light shall see, in evening's breath,
My banner wave in victory, and give it greeting fair,

Or it shall see my silent face set pale and cold in death.

Part II

The Song of the Knight

Siamanto (Atom Yarjanian) was born at Akn, Asia Minor, in 1878, of prosperous parents, who later moved to Constantinople. He was well educated. Abdul Hamid's massacres made a deep impression on him. He sympathized with the revolutionary movement, and left Constantinople. Thrown upon his own resources by his father's death, he led the life of a poor student in Paris, Vienna, Zurich and Lausanne. When the new constitution was proclaimed in Turkey, he returned to Constantinople, devoted himself to writing, and supported his younger brothers and sisters. A volume of poems published in 1902 under the pen name of Siamanto had made him famous, and other volumes followed. After the Adana massacres he came to America and spent a year in Boston, editing the Armenian paper Hairenik. He then returned to Constantinople, and he is believed to have been among the group of educated and influential Armenians of that city who were massacred in 1915, after barbarous tortures. Siamanto was a man of lovable character, and is considered one of the greatest Armenian poets.

The sun is up, the hour has come for starting, O my steed!
A moment wait till I pass my foot through thy stirrup glittering clear.

I read my Aim in thy shining eyes, that know and understand.
Oh, joy of joys! Oh, blest be thou, my steed, my steed so dear!

My body still is firm and light with the joy and spring of youth,
And on thy saddle I shall perch like an eagle, proud and free.
The golden oats that I gave to thee in plenty, O my steed!
Have made mad life through thy form flame up; how fleet thy course will be!

Galloping thou wilt fly along, fly ever upon thy way.
And sparks from the strokes of thy brazen shoes will blossom as we go past.
Let us grow drunk with our rapid course like heroes, O my steed!
And, infinitely winged like the wind, drink in the blast!

The boundless space before thy pace recedes and disappears,
The sinful cities with all their crimes bow down beneath thy tread.
Black flocks of crows that tremble thy swiftness to behold
Are seeking shelter in the clouds, the thick clouds overhead.

The sad earth seems below us and we up among the stars;
Thou no abyss nor downward slope dost heed, with eyes aflame;

There is no obstacle, no rock that can thy flight impede;

Impatient, fain wouldst thou attain the summit of the Aim.

My fleet, fleet steed! My idol of snow-white marble fair!

With all my soul I worship thee! As on our course we fly,
My dreamy brow is burning with the flames of mine Ideal;

Oh, spur me onward to my Aim! Slave of thy footsteps I!

I am the slave of thy fleet steps, child of the hurricane!

Speed on, athirst for vengeance, O swift, swift steed of mine!
A needless halt I spurn and hate, with all my anger's might.

Ours are the summits, and the wreath of victory is thine!

Thy delicate cream-white body boils with thine ardent fire of life;

Thy tail is a cataract; rushing down, like a hurricane it blows.
Within thine eyes, so bright and keen, there shine two flaming stars;

The ring of thy swift shoes forges fear, as onward our journey goes.

I told thee that I am thy slave, for liberty athirst.

Oh, bear me swiftly toward the South, away from this frontier!

We shall be clothed with suns and blood, beyond the stately heights

Of Ararat and Aragatz. Speed on, my courser dear!

I hold no whip within my hand, my courser, thou art free;

Upon thy back, that glistens like a lily white and fair,
I only shed sweet touches of my fingers as we go.

They touch thy bright flesh like a stream of honey dropping there.

Thou hast no bridle upon thy neck, no bit within thy mouth;

Enough for me one wave of hair from thy full mane backward flung.
I have no need of stirrup-irons for my feet to grip thy sides;

A silver saddle thou hast alone, a saddle with pearls bestrung.

For my native valleys I yearn, I yearn, the valleys that hold my home,

But halt thou never, my courser swift, the star-strewn heavens below!
Away by the mouths of caverns deep like a shadow thou must pass,

From forests, vineyards and gardens green still farther and farther go.

Who knows, perchance a maiden fair by the side of a running brook

Might hand me a cluster of golden grapes, and proffer a draught of wine;

My soul might understand her, and she like a
sister smile on me —
   But I do not wish to be lost in dreams; halt
not, swift steed of mine!

Thou wilt pass by the shadowy bowers of my
birthplace, Eden-fair;
   The nightingale, the nightingale, fain
would I drink her song!
The rose-scent, on my pilgrimage, I have
dreamed of many a year.
   Oh, how my heart is yearning! But halt
not, speed along.

And in my pathway haply old corpses might
arise,
   Their shrouds upon their shoulders, their
hands held out to me,
Approach me — me the wretched! — and
breathe upward to mine ear
   Their loves and vengeance ne'er to be for-
got — but onward flee!

I shudder at the ruins and at barren, helpless
pangs.
   My courser, near the ashes of the cities
make no stay!
Oh, tears, the tears of others, they choke me
without ruth;
   The woe, the griefs of others drive me
mad, upon my way!

Oh, do not halt, my courser, where these
corpses scattered lie!
   Fly far away from graveyards, where white
shades of dead men be.

I cannot bear, I tell thee, I cannot bear again
   The death of my dear native land with
anguished eyes to see!

Behold the landscape of the place in which I
had my birth!
   At sight of it my longing glance with tears
grows moist and glows.
But yet I would not shed them; nay, do not
pause or stay,
   My steed, my steed of swiftest flight! My
Aim no weakness knows.

Lo! 'tis Euphrates sounding. Why, river, dost
thou roar?
   Thy son is passing. Why so dark the flood
thy shore that laves?
I am thy son. Oh, do not rage! Hast thou
forgotten me?
   I with thy current would speed on, and
would outstrip thy waves.

The memory of my childhood draws from
me tears of blood;
   A dreamy youth who used to stray along
these banks of thine.
All full of hope, with sunlight mad, and hap-
py with his dreams —
   But ah! what am I saying? Pause not, swift
steed of mine!

Behold the glorious autumn, which vaguely
dies around!
   Upon my brow a yellow leaf has fallen like
a dream.

Is it my death it stands for, or the crowning of my faith?

What matter? On, my neighing steed, sweep onward with the stream!

Perchance it was the last sere leaf of my ill-omened fate

That fell upon us even now. What matter? Speed away!

From the four corners of the land are echoing the words,

"Ideal, O free-born Ideal, halt not, halt not nor stay!"

I worship thee! Now like a star thou shootest on thy course;

Thou art as fleet, thou art as free, as is the lightning's flame;

And through the wind and with the wind like eagles now we soar.

I am thy knight, I am thy slave; oh, lift me to my Aim!

Down from the summits of the rocks, the dread and cloudy peaks.

The cataracts, the cataracts are falling in their might!

Their currents white are pure, my steed, as thine own snow-white form.

And their imperious downward sweep is savage as thy flight.

But why now doth a shudder through all thy body run?

Oh, what has chanced, my hero? Why do thy looks grow dark?

Oh, turn thine eyes away from me, thine eyes with trouble filled;

Past the horizons fly along, fly like a wind-borne bark!

I heard the wailing and the cries, entreaties and laments,

From ruined huts and cities that reached us on our way.

But ah! what use in pausing all powerless before pain?

Our task is to relieve it; then do not halt nor stay.

Through the death-agony, my steed, we passed with tearless eyes.

Oh, do not halt! Oh, do not stay! Brave be that heart of thine!

From this time onward, I will burn Hope's torches blazing bright.

To halt means death to us; pause not, O gallant steed of mine!

Aloft on thy galloping form, full oft, in our journey ere to-day

I have heard how thy swift, spark-scattering hoofs, as ever we forward l1ec.

Have many and many a time crushed bones, that fell beneath their tread.

And the skulls with their empty sockets dark gazed at me — didst thou see?

I tell thee, under thy shoes I heard the skeletons break and crash.

But I kept silence. My lips are dumb. Halt not, halt not, my steed!

66

I will bury my sobs and sighs of grief in my soul's abysmal depths.

Let nothing live but my anger hot! Pause not, but onward speed!

Oh, pause not, falter not in thy course, wild creature of marble white!

Tears will not banish the Pain of Life, nor drive out its woe and wrong.
Nay, the Ideal shall toll, shall toll the bells of glowing wrath.

The cranes, far flying, will call to us; oh, follow their distant song!

But where does thy path lead? What is this? My steed, hast thou lost thy mind?

The ashes! Oh, the desolate plains of ashes and ruins gray!
Like fog the gray dust rises up to stifle and choke our breath.

Oh, tear thy way through these frightful mounds, break through them and speed away!

Lift up thy forehead, lift up thine eyes, let me cover them with my hand!

Halt not, 'tis the Crimson, the Crimson dread; red blood beneath us lies.
Across my face to blind mine eyes I have pulled my fluttering scarf;

Halt not! What good would it do, my steed, to pause here with useless sighs?

Ah, once, accompanied by my griefs, my lyre shed tears of blood;

Weeping I hate from this time on; thou only art my soul.
Thou breathest battle, for glory keen, and I am thy prince, thy slave!

Thy form was worshipped by glorious Greece. Oh, lift me to my Goal!

The sound of the wind is like a horn that is winded far away;

The forests, ranged like troops of war, stood ready as we passed.
At the wild ringing of thy hoofs, old hopes like giants woke;

Old laws are crushed, old tears are shed, old sounds are dying fast.

And in thy flight, at daybreak, on a lofty table-land.

New giants, new insurgents, new heroes we shall spy.
The sons of suffering are they, who in this hostile age

Were born in blood, are wroth with blood, and wish in blood to die.

When we see columns rolling up, armed with the hurricane,

We by their side will march along the pathway to the Aim.
Of glory and the crowning of the martyrs I shall sing;

My lyre will play, that gallant day, my Torches burn and flame!

The day has dawned, has dawned at last! I am thy knight, thy slave!

The slope is difficult and steep, but, breath-
ing heavily,
Thou must fly on — one effort more, amid
the fires of morn!
   I am athirst for victory, my noble steed,
like thee.

A few more ringing steps, my steed, and one
last bound! and then
   What a procession, what a host, all glad
and full of might!
'Tis Freedom's pioneers; their swords flash
out life-giving rays.
   And Brotherhood they celebrate in morn-
ing's glorious light.

Here may'st thou halt. Be blest, my steed!
Worthy of God art thou!
   Tears fill my soul as mine Ideal I gaze on
and admire.
Thy triumph is the mighty law of beauty
infinite.
   Lo, there six sombre centuries are standing,
armed with fire!

I, armed already, will arm thee. O'er my
shoulder burns thy torch.
   They like the tempest wish to walk, under
the dawning's glow,
Laden with justice. Oh, the land is barren
and athirst!
   Lo, from our flight the giant Hope sparks
in the paths will sow!

The Mother's Dream

Let me write now and tell you of my dream.
It was upon the midnight of All Saints.
Sudden before me your four brothers knelt;
They wore no shrouds, no vestiges of flesh;
Groping in darkness, with abysmal eyes,
Weeping before their mother thus they came
To tell their memories of other days.

"Mother, the dawning of the bygone days!
We four together, from beneath the ground,
Today have sought once more your little
door
To tap on it, companioned by the storm.
Mother, be not afraid, no strangers we!
And, lonely in your slumber, wait at least
And let us watch your face in death's dark
night!"

"Mother, the holiness of bygone days!
Out of my heart, 'neath our poor graveyard's
earth,
Mother, a flower of love for you has grown!"

"Mother, the sweetness of the bygone days!
For you two jars with my salt tears are filled."

"Mother, the happiness of bygone days!
For you have burning roses, flowers of hope,
Sprung into fiery blossom from my soul!"

"O mother, the heroic manliness
Of bygone days! Out of my breast -bones
now
Two shields for your protection have been
wrought."

"Mother, your peerless beauty in the past!
How many furrows now have marked your brow!"
(Thus spake your eldest brother). "All alone
Under your roof-tree, how can you endure?
These seven years, we seven times have tapped
Upon your little door, but till to-night
We never yet have found the door unclosed.
What traveler do you await to-night?
Behold, your fragile hut is tottering,
Like to a heap of mouldering coffin-boards.
See how the leaves, storm-rent, fall from the trees!
The guiltless doves are dying in the brook.
And still upon the threshold of your home.
Mother, the black snakes lick our dried-up blood.
The garden has no leaf, no fruit, no brier.
We four together have been through the hut,
And at the sight of us our broken swords
Gave out once more a single flash of light.
Empty the larder was, and in the barn
A white lamb bleated, biting at its hoofs.
Mother, the plenty of the bygone days!
The love and pity of the bygone days!
How can you live here in your empty hut.
Here in your empty hut how can you live?"

The four were mute; but when I spoke your name
And sobbed tempestuously in my dream,
They wildly, with bowed heads, began to weep.
"But still," I said, "your brother is alive —
The little one, who did not see you die.

It is for him alone I live to-day."

Then they burst forth, and poured upon mine eyes
The terrible black tear drops of the dead.
"A brother, oh, we have a brother yet,
A brother, oh, a brother in the world!
Mother, the misery of coming days!
Hereafter, how shall we to earth return?
Now how, oh, how shall we to earth return?"

Prayer

The swans, in discouragement, have migrated
from the poisonous lakes this evening,
And sad sisters dream of brothers under the
prison walls.
Battles have ended on the blossoming fields
of lilies,
And fair women follow coffins from under-
ground passages,
And sing, with heads bowed down towards
the ground.

Oh, make haste! Our aching bodies are fro-
zen in these pitiless glooms.
Make haste towards the chapel, where life
will be more merciful,
The chapel of the graveyard where our
brother sleeps!

An orphan swan is suffering within my soul,
And there, over newly-buried bodies,
It rains blood — it pours from mine eyes.

A crowd of cripples pass along the paths of my heart.
And with them pass barefooted blind men,
In the divine hope of meeting some one in prayer.
And the red dogs of the desert howled all one night,
After hopelessly moaning over the sands
For some unknown, incomprehensible grief.

And the storm of my thoughts ceased with the rain;
The waves were cruelly imprisoned under the frozen waters;
The leaves of huge oaks, like wounded birds.
Dropped with cries of anguish.

And the dark night was deserted, like the vast infinite;
And, with the lonely and bloody moon,
Like a myriad motionless marble statues.
All the dead bodies of our earth arose to pray for one another.

My Tears

I was alone with my pure-winged dream in the valleys my sires had trod;
My steps were light as the fair gazelle's, and my heart with joy was thrilled;
I ran, all drunk with the deep blue sky, with the light of the glorious days;
Mine eyes were filled with gold and hopes, my soul with the gods was filled.

Basket on basket, the Summer rich presented her fruit to me
From my garden's trees — each kind of fruit that to our clime belongs;
And then from a willow's body slim, melodious, beautiful,
A branch for my magic flute I cut in silence, to make my songs.

I sang; and the brook all diamond bright, and the birds of my ancient home,
And the music pure from heavenly wells that fills the nights and days.
And the gentle breezes and airs of dawn, like my sister's soft embrace,
United their voices sweet with mine, and joined in my joyous lays.

To-night in a dream, sweet flute, once more I took you in my hand;
You felt to my lips like a kiss — a kiss from the days of long ago.
But when those memories old revived, then straightway failed my breath,
And instead of songs, my tears began drop after drop to flow.

The Young Wife's Dream

Year after year, sitting alone at my window,
I gaze on thy path, my pilgrim heart-mate,
And by this writing I wish once more to sing
The tremors of my body and mind, left without a guardian.

Ah! dost thou not recall the sun on the day of thy departure?

My tears were so plentiful and my kisses so ardent.

Thy promises were so good and thy return was to be so early!

Dost thou not recall the sun and my prayers on the day of thy departure,

When I sprinkled water on the shadow of thy steed from my water-jar,

That the seas might open before thee.

And the earth might bloom beneath thy feet?

Ah, the sun of the day of thy departure has changed to black night,

And the tears of waiting, beneath the shower of so many years,

Have poured from mine eyes like stars on my cheeks,

And behold! their roses have withered.

It is enough. Through longing for thee, I feel like plucking out my hair;

I am still under the influence of the wine of thy cup,

And a mourner for thy absent superb stature;

And, wounding my knees with kneeling at the church door,

I entreat for thee, turning towards the west.

Let the seas some day dry up from shore to shore.

And let the two worlds approach each other in an instant!

Then I should have no need of heaven or of the sun.

Return! I am waiting for thy return on the threshold of our cottage.

My hands empty of thy hands, I dream of thee, in my black robes.

Return, like the sweet fruits of our garden!

My heart's love keeps my kiss for thee.

Oh, my milk-white hips have not yet known motherhood,

And I have not yet been able to decorate a swaddling cloth

With my wedding veil, wrought with golden thread;

And I have not yet been able to sing, sitting beside a cradle,

The pure, heavenly lullaby of Armenian mothers.

Return! My longing has no end,

When the black night comes thus to unfold its shrouds.

When the owls in the courtyard shriek with one another.

When my sobs end and my tears become bloody.

Lonely in my dreams of a despairing bride,

With my hands, like a demon, I begin

To sift upon my head the earth of my grave, which is drawing near to me.

Thirst

My soul is listening to the death of the twilight.

Kneeling on the far-away soil of suffering, my soul is drinking the wounds of twilight and of the ground; and within itself it feels the raining down of tears.

And all the stars of slaughtered lives, so like to eyes grown dim, in the pools of my heart this evening are dying of despair and of waiting.

And the ghosts of all the dead to-night will wait for the dawn with mine eyes and my soul. Perhaps, to satisfy their thirst for life, a drop of light will fall upon them from on high.

The Starving

O ye ancient and undisturbed Armenian plains of kind mornings,
And ye, golden fields, rich orchards, and pastures smiling with life.
Ye valleys covered with marble, flower-beds and kind and fruitful gardens —
Ye that create wine, which causes self-forgetfulness, and eternal, sacred daily bread!
Ye indescribable paradises of plants, birds, flowers and songs!
To-day, once more, at the lonely hour of my returning memory, of my sorrowful grief and delirium,
I call on your spirits, in bitterness live your life, and hopelessly weep for you!

Out of the blue, boundless space the fiery dawns open their lilies,
And lo! the proud cock makes his silvery voice resound.

The kotchnaks [1] click from village to village;
An harmonious flute joyously announces invitations;
And the herds scatter themselves over the hilltops.
With the dance of the industrious and busy bees.
And the peace sings. The flowers tremble. The buds seem to have the glances of saintly women.
Art thou reminded of the white voice of the flour-mill, the ever-moving body of fertility and labor,
Which turns its obedient and tireless wheel by the billows of the unbridled torrent of the valley,
Apportioning the blessing of its flour to the cities and villages, from time immemorial?

The brooks flow through the velvet mosses like children's nakedness;
The morning smoke of fireplaces and chimneys alike pours out its incense.
The beautiful young women with marble breasts go, pitcher in hand, to the springs for the diamond-pure water.
Others draw near the rosebush, to sing with the nightingale of their new-born love.

It is the happy climate of the harvest, full of good tidings, that is born.
Nature is pregnant, and the farmers, who have drunk of the fruit and effort of their skill.

72

Crowd around the plains. The scythes on their shoulders flash like hope.
Andastan [2] is about to begin. To-day is the dawn of the harvest's blessing.

Let a prayer for nature, for beneficent nature, rise from men's lips!
May the soil grant its innumerable ears of wheat to us, and to humanity in the four corners of the earth, —
To the neighbor, to the friend, to the enemy, to the evil man and to the stranger!
Let all hunger be appeased, and let all thirst be quenched with the bright water!

This celebration is solemnized from north to south, from east to west,
For the abundance of every race, every class, every caste, every field and every harvest.
Prayers are solemnized, and sweetened, and purified; and out of the mist of incense
Smiles of joy brighten the face of the good peasant with sunny hope.

The ears still standing kiss one another once more with thoughts of the wind;
The sickles move, and golden seas, seas, seas are being mown;
And sheaves, bundle by bundle, through the shadows of the fertile evening.
Like a multitude of stars that have rained down, meditate motionless from field to field.

The day is done; and with the blooming rose and the songs of early morn,

Huge oxen, pair by pair, around the threshing rings will thresh the wonderful wheat.
The flour mills will work, the thoner [3] will burn.
Behold all significance, all reason, all law, purpose, cleanliness and greatness of incomprehensible life!

O all ye strange thoughts of my suffering, avaunt for this evening!

- - - - - -

My unhappy dream in ashes disclosed its wounded aspect.
See! the endless golden fields of yesterday wear the terrible appearance of graveyards,
And the waters of ruined fountains, so like the tears of a dying man,
Join the sobbing brooks, and go to moisten the black aspect of the horrible ruins.

In place of the infinite goodness of ears of wheat, yellow thistles have sprung up.
And over the fruit-bearing gardens the dark cawing of black crows is dying away.
With their arms outstretched against the horizon, gaunt and frail trees
With the rising of the winds are crushed against one another, like the skeletons of countless dead.
The ill-omened tempest flies along the paths by night with roaring as of a forest,
Demolishing half-ruined villages and roofs beneath the anger of its sweep,
Opening earth-mounds and graves, strangling birds in the caves.

Meanwhile from the caverns the howling of the devouring wild beasts tolls the knell of death.

There is no harvest, no harvester, no sower and no earth to plow.
Hungry oxen bellow mournfully. Vegetation is dying with the flowers.
The plow in the corner of the barn awaits the new and never-returning spring.
The cock crows no more. The dawn, it seems, like the blood of my race, has sunk into the depths of the earth.

The innumerable caravans of wretchedness, from every side, migrate towards the plains;
Tragically beating their breasts, they frame, prayers, hoping against hope.
They celebrate the fields of bygone dawns, they implore, they bleed.
"O Lord, we are hungry, have pity on us!
Nature, have pity on us! Men, we are hungry! Humanity, we are hungry!"

The current of water carries the corpse of the miller.
And the mad flour-mill turns vainly, like an empty coffin.
Grinding the horror, the wailing, the death of all that surrounds it.
Madly it turns, gnawing at its millstone and wheels.

The new-born babes, with terrible eyes, suck the dry breasts.

Oh, the vision of Armenian mothers, the nearly-blinded eyes of the mothers before all these!
Oh, where is the road, where is the abyss, whore is forgetfulness, where is the awful pit?
But death does not come, it does not come.
Like the longed-for salvation, it does not come.

The tremulous old women, groaning beneath their head-coverings.
Amid the ashes of their ruined homes, at sunrise, with savage blood all around them,
Among the ashes of their fallen homes, kneeling diligently before their wooden kneading-troughs.
Bake in haste a little bread for the starving ones.

And the miserable throng of beggars with shattered bodies
Wander along the painful road like phantoms,
And, though disheartened with knocking at the doors of enemies, friends and pious folk,
They once more return, again shed tears, once more beg, once more suffer the agonies of death.

Hear this sobbing, supplication, begging!
"We are hungry, we are hungry!"
There are those who tear their hair, there are those who shed tears like drops of lead.
There are those who hope they are already dead under cover of a pall of silence,

74

There are those who once more dig the hard earth with their bleeding nails.
There are those who fall one upon another in the graves,
There are those who still look for plants and roots with stubborn hope.
There are those who begin horribly to dance, arm in arm with frightful madness;
And others, terrible to tell, already approach the corpses, unburied and awaiting burial.

O ye hostile thoughts of my suffering, avaunt, all of ye, upon this evening!

[1] The kotchnak is a small wooden board that is beaten with a stick to arouse the sleepers.
[2] Andastan corresponds to our Thanksgiving Day.
[3] The thoner is a round, open fireplace built in the ground.

The Longing Letter

Daniel Varoujan was born in a village of Sebastia in 1884. He studied at St. Lazare, Venice, and later in Belgium. He is the author of a series of martial and patriotic epics. He is believed to have perished in the Constantinople massacres of 1915.

My mother writes: "My son on pilgrimage,
    How long beneath a strange moon will you roam?
How long a time must pass ere your poor head
    To my warm bosom I may press, at home?

"Oh, long enough upon strange stairs have trod
    Your feet, which in my palms I warmed one day —
Your heart, in which my breasts were emptied once,
    Far from my empty heart has pined away!

"My arms are weary at the spinning wheel;
    I weave my shroud, too, with my hair of snow.
Ah, would mine eyes could see you once again,
    Then close forever, with my heart below!

"Always I sit in sadness at my door.
    And tidings ask from every crane that flies.
That willow slip you planted long ago
    Has grown till over me its shadow lies.

"I wait in vain for your return at eve.
    All the brave fellows of the village pass,
The laborer goes by, the herdsman bold —
    I with the moon am left alone, alas!

"My ruined house is left without a head.
    Sometimes for death, and always for the cheer
Of my own hearth I yearn. A tortoise I,
    Whose entrails to its broken shell adhere!

"Oh, come, my son, your ancient home restore!
    They burst the door, they swept the larders bare.

75

Now all the swallows of the spring come in
  Through shattered windows, open to the air.

"Of all the goodly flocks of long ago
  One brave ram only in our stable stands.
His mother once — remember, little son —
  While yet a lamb, ate oats out of your hands.

"Rice, bran and clover fine I give him now,
  To nourish his rich dmak, [1] of noble size;
I comb his soft wool with a wooden comb;
  He is a dear and precious sacrifice.

"When you come back, his head with roses wreathed,
  He shall be sacrificed to feast you, sweet;
And in his blood, my well-beloved son,
  I then will wash my pilgrim's weary feet."

[1] A mass of fat which hangs down behind sheep of this breed, in place of a tail.

The Working Girl

Beneath my window, as each morning dawns,
You like a wandering ghost go flitting by.
And on your beauteous virgin head there fall
Tears from my rose vine, leafless now and dry.

I hear your footsteps in the silent street,
And the awakened dog that barks at you;
Or in my sleep I hear the constant cough
That racks your lovely bosom through and through.

I think that you are hungry, robbed of sleep.
Your body shivering in the breezes cold.
And on your tresses, O my sister! lies
The frost, like jewels, glittering to behold.

Or else, I think, your shoes are torn and rent;
The water from the street is oozing through;
Or impudently, as you pass along.
Some scoundrel Turk is whistling after you.

I think that ill at home your mother lies,
And that the oil which fed the lamp is dry,
And to the factory you go, to toil
For light and life.   I think of it, and sigh!

I think of it, and madly then I wish
I might come down, my pallid sister dear,
Come down to you, to kiss your thin, frail hand,
And whisper low, "I love you!" in your ear.

I love your sorrow, which is mine as well —
My grief of griefs, all other woes above;
I love your shattered breast, where still your love
Sings on and on — a skylark wild with love.

Pale girl, I long to press you to my heart
Like some poor banished dove, forlorn and lone —
Give you my strength, my prizes won from fame.
And my untarnished name to be your own.

Fain would I be your honor's veil and screen.
My breast a shield for your defenceless breast.
If I could guard, with arms as granite strong.
Your sex and your grave beauty, I were blest!

Fain would I give you all that I have won
In life's hard struggle, all I have of good —
Crown you with roses of my victory,
Roses that wear the color of my blood;

Only that never more, my sister dear.
You should be pale and hungry, coughing sore,
And that your mother's lamp should not go out.
And to the factory you should go no more!

Alms to the Starving People

"There is famine; bread, bread!"
Who is sighing?
On the threshold of my cottage, who is sighing?
My love has gone out, with the flame in my fireplace.
Ashes within me, ashes around me; oh, of what use is it
To sow tears on ashes?
I have nothing, nothing! To-day, with my last
Small coin I bought poison;
I shall mix poison within me.
Come to-morrow to the graveyard, thou Hungry One,

Through the storm, early, when around the village
Wolves are still wandering.
Come to-morrow! As bread, from my grave
I will throw into that bag of thine
My poet's heart.
My poet's heart shall be thy blood, the blood of thy orphans.
As long as thy grief lives.
Come to-morrow to the graveyard, O thou Hungry One!

The Aged Crane

On the bank of the river, in the row of cranes,
That one drooped its head.
Put its beak under its wing, and with its aged
Dim pupils, awaited
Its last black moment.
When its comrades wished to depart.
It could not join them in their flight.
Scarcely could it open its eyes and watch in the air
The path of the little flock that went along
Calling down to those under the roofs
The tidings, the greetings and the tears
Entrusted to them by the exile.
Ah, the poor bird! In the bleak embrace
Of that cold autumnal silence, it is dying.
It is vain to dream any more
Of a distant spring, of cool currents of air
Under strong and soaring wings.
Or of passing through cool brooks
With naked feet, of dipping its long neck

Amongst the green reeds;
It is vain to dream any more!
The wings of the Armenian crane
Are tired of traveling. It was true
To its heart-depressing calling;
It has transported so many tears!
How many young wives have put among its soft feathers
Their hearts, ardently beating!
How many separated mothers and sons
Have loaded its wings with kisses!
Now, with a tremor on its dying day,
It shakes from its shoulders
The vast sorrow of an exiled race.
The vows committed to it, the hidden sighs
Of a betrothed bride who saw at length
Her last rose wither unkissed;
A mother's sad blessing;
Loves, desires, longings.
It shakes at last from its shoulders.
And on the misty river-bank
Its weary wings, spread for the last time,
Point straight toward
The Armenian hills, the half-ruined villages.
With the voice of its dying day
It curses immigration.
And falls, in silence, upon the coarse sand of the river bank.
It chooses its grave.
And, thrusting its purple beak
Under a rock, the dwelling-place of a lizard,
Stretching out its curving neck
Among the songs of the waves.
With a noble tremor it expires!

A serpent there, which had watched that death-agony
Silently for a long time with staring pupils,
Crawls up from the river-bank,
And, to revenge a grudge of olden days,
With an evil and swift spring
Coils around its dead neck.

The Bond

Archag Tchobanian was born in Constantinople in 1872, the son of a poor silversmith. He became a teacher and writer, contributing to various periodicals poems, fairy tales, literary studies and criticisms. He brought out a successful drama, was appointed teacher of the history of literature in the Central School, and became editor of a literary and artistic magazine. In 1895 he settled in Paris, where he has devoted himself to making the Armenians better known in Europe. He is an indefatigable worker, and has published, in French, a number of volumes containing translations of Armenian literature, ancient and modern, besides editing "Anahit," a literary and critical magazine which he founded.

All things are bound together by a tie
    Finer and subtler than a ray of light;
Color and sound and fleeting fragrances,
    The maiden's smile, the star-beam sparkling bright,
Are knit together by a secret bond
    Finer and subtler than a ray of light.

Sometimes an urn of memories is unsealed

Just by a simple tune, or sad or gay;
Part of the past with every quivering note
   From its dark sleep awakens to the day.
And we live o'er again a long-past life,
   Just through a simple tune, or sad or gay.

Some flowers bring men and women back to mind;
   A well-known face smiles on us in their hue;
Their bright cups, moved by the capricious wind.
   Will make us dream of eyes, black eyes or blue;
We in their fragrance feel a breath beloved;
   Flowers bring back men and women whom we knew.

The summer sea recalls fond, happy hours;
   We in the sunset see our dead once more;
In starlight, holy loves upon us smile;
   With our own griefs the stormy thunders roar;
The zephyr breathes to us a name adored;
   We in the sunset see the dead once more.

All things are bound in closest unison,
   Throughout the world, by many a mystic thread.
The flower, and love, the breeze and reverie.
   Nature and man, and things alive and dead,
Are all akin, and bound in harmony
   Throughout the world, by many a mystic thread.

To The Moon

Why am I not the thin white cloud
   That, floating soft and slow,
Veils the pure splendor of your face
   'Neath its transparent snow?

Or one of those unnumbered stars —
   Bees that in heaven's height
Flit round you, seeking honey there,
   O shining Rose of light?

Why am I not the dark-browed mount
   Where you a moment stay,
Ere spreading your broad, viewless wings
   To soar through heaven away?

Why am I not the forest deep,
   Where, dropping through the air,
'Mid foliage dark slip in and hang
   Threads of your golden hair?

Why am I not the tranquil sea
   On which your beams descend,
Where molten diamonds and fire
   And milk and honey blend?

Alas, why am I not at least
   That cold tomb of the dead,
On which your rays so tenderly
   Their tears' bright sadness shed?

The Wind

The Wind's the aged traveler
   Who sings old songs he knows,
As all alone, without a guide,
   He through the forest goes.

His voice caresses like a kiss
   When over flowers he strays;
The Wind's the ancient traveler
   Who murmurs old-time lays.

But like a cataract he roars
   Far out upon the sea,
And rushing through the winter nights
   He curses savagely.

Within My Heart

Within my heart there is a maid
   Would fain, with earnest will,
Recall an old, forgotten tune;
   But it eludes her still.

Within my heart there is a child
   Who waits, with longing dumb
And endless hope, for somebody
   Who does not, does not come.

There is an old man in my heart
   Who calls eternally
To someone very far away
   Who never makes reply.

Lullaby for Mother Armenia

All naked at the crossroads thou dost sit.
The snow descends and clings along thine hair.
Dark wounds are in thy flesh; thine eyes have grown
As red as lakes of blood, in thy despair.

The ancient Mother thou, of age-long griefs;
Misfortune round thy heart its chain hath laid
In countless rings; black winds have smitten thee,
And heavy shadows on thy life have weighed.

What evil fairy spun thy thread of fate?
Who, seeing thee cast down and like to die,
Will call to mind that thou wast once a maid
Of mighty strength, with proud and radiant eye?

Thy tresses like a banner floated wide
On the free mountain where thy spirit fleet
Leaped, with exultant cry, from peak to peak;
Thy proud breast swelled with milk as honey sweet.

All brigands have desired thee; monstrous foes
Threw themselves on thee; long didst thou contend,
Long didst thou struggle, until, wearied out,
Thou didst sink down exhausted at the end.

And yet, amid destructive forces vast,
Thy soul was kind and fruitful in all worth.
Thou to the world didst add a flower of life;
Thy fingers drew forth beauty from the earth.

Mother of gold wast thou, with dazzling breasts, —
The Goddess Anahit, [1] with peaceful eyes.
Wealth from thy bosom rained, rays from thy glance;
Thy lips were musical, thy hands were wise.

Barbarians bound thy hands, thy tender flesh
Tore and polluted; in those darksome days
Thou didst become the Mother blood-bestained,
With myriad wounds, and dragged through Calvary's ways.

Yet thou wast beauteous, thou wast brave in pain!
In fetters, still thy soul did ardent burn.
Thou brokest many a formidable yoke,
And oft from death to life didst thou return.

Thine eyes were turned forever to the light;
Toward the new world its course thy spirit sped;
And thou stood'st firm for centuries, all alone,
Against the flood of Asia making head.

That torrent, growing greater and more fierce,
O'erthrew thee, quenched beneath its waves thy light.
Then wretched, panting, stretched upon the earth,

Yet living still, thou waitedst through the night.

Sometimes by night the crosses of old tombs
Stirred and were shaken; with an angry light
The genii of Mt. Ararat passed by;
From thy great lakes shot flashes red and bright.

The low sound of a drum-beat crossed the air,
And, trembling, to the mountain summit bold
Thou didst lift up thine eyes; then fell again
The heavy shadows and the silence cold.

Once, anguished, thou upstartedst; from thy lips
A cry of pain and of rebellion rushed;
But deaf the world remained; thine effort vain
'Neath the blind heel of brutal force was crushed.

'Mid fires of evil omen, monsters dire
Appeared, which burned thine heart, plucked out thine eyes.
Driven from thy home, thou on the ground didst fall
'Mid blood and ashes, 'neath the windy skies.

And now, a mournful shadow, thou dost sit
'Mid smoking ruins, desolate, oppressed.
Thy wounds are bitten by the wind; the blood
Falls drop by drop from thy discolored breast.

Slowly thou shak'st thy head, and shedding tears
Thou singest low and sweet a lullaby —
That of thy children fallen in their blood,
Or exiled, scattered, flung abroad to die;

The lullaby of youthful flames now quenched,
And eyes now darkened that were once so fair;
And that of those who live and suffer still,
In poverty, in dungeons, in despair.

Enough! Thy lullaby's a chant of death!
Enough! We'll sing thee a new lullaby —
A lullaby of hope and of revenge.
The dead will thrill with joy where low they lie.

Lift up thy head, weep not! Holy is grief,
And great and wholesome. Earth naught nobler knows
Than is the victim brave beneath his cross.
'Tis in the shadow that the dawn-light grows.

The black destroyers, the red torturers
Shall vanish — they like smoke shall disappear.
And from thine ashes thou shalt rise again,
Made young by suffering, radiant, bright and clear.

Weep not! No longer droop thy piteous head.
Nor let thine hair stream wild the winds among;
But know thyself, and gather up thy powers!

Thy strength has propped a stranger's house too long.

Pale brothers who have fallen, sleep in peace!
Stretch thy great hands and bless us, Mother! Rise,
And may our blood dry up, and may our lives
Be for thine happiness a sacrifice!

Thou shalt come forth triumphant from these shades;
Stars shall thine eyes become, and sparkle bright;
Thy wounds to radiant roses shall be changed,
And from thy whitened hair shall spring forth light.

Thou at the opening of the ways shalt stand,
And break the bonds that held thee down in gloom.
O Mother, rise! thy pains were childbirth pangs;
It is a world that stirs within thy womb!

[1] The Goddess of love, in Armenia's pagan days.

When Some Day

Hovhannes Toumanian was born in a village of Lorga in 1869. He received little schooling, but has educated himself. His poems are very popular; and he is also the author of many translations. Since the late massacres he has been active and tireless in the relief work.

Sweet comrade, when you come some day
  To gaze upon my tomb,
And scattered all around it see
  Bright flowers in freshest bloom,

Think not that those are common flowers
  Which at your feet are born,
Or that the spring has brought them there
  My new home to adorn.

They are my songs unsung, which used
  Within my heart to hide;
They are the words of love I left
  Unuttered when I died.

They are my ardent kisses, dear,
  Sent from that world unknown,
The path to which before you lies
  Blocked by the tomb alone!

Before a Painting by Ayvasovsky

Rising from ocean, billows uncontrolled,
With heavy flux and reflux, beating high,
Towered up like mountains, roaring terribly;
The wild storm blew with wind gusts mani-
fold -
A mad, tempestuous race
Through endless, boundless space.

"Halt!" cried the aged wizard, brush in hand,
To the excited elements; and lo!
Obedient to the voice of genius, now
The dark waves, in the tempest's fury grand,
Upon the canvas, see!
Stand still eternally!

In The Cottage

The little children wept and wailed;
  Heart-rending were the tears they shed.
"Mamma, mamma, we want our foodiv
  Get up, mamma, and give us bread!"

With bitter sorrow in her heart
  Groaned the sick mother from her bed:
"We have no bread, my little ones;
  Papa has gone to get you bread."

"No, you are cheating, bad mamma!
  You are deceiving us! You said
That when the sunlight struck the banks
  Papa would come and bring us bread.

"The sun has come, the sun has gone;
  Still are we hungry, still unfed.
Mamma, mamma, we want our food!
  Get up, mamma, and give us bread!"

"No bread your father yet has found;
  Without it he dares not come back.
Wait but a little while, my dears!
  Now I will follow in his track.

"In heaven there is a great Papa;
  Abundant store of bread has he.
He loves you much, so very much,
  He will not let you hungry be.

"There will I go and say to him
  That you are faint with hunger sore.
Plenty of bread I'll ask for you,
  That you may eat, and weep no more."

So spake the mother, and she clasped
  The starving children to her breast.
On her pale lips the last kiss froze
  That to their faces thin she pressed.

The mother's arms unclosed no more —
  She shut her eyes and went away
Bread to her little ones to send —
  And lifeless in their sight she lay.

The little children wept and wailed;
  Heart-rending were the tears they shed.
"Mamma, mamma, we want our food;
  Get up, mamma, and give us bread!"

New Spring

Hovhannes Hovhannessian, teacher and writer, was born in 1864 at Vagharshabad, near Etchmiadzin. He is a graduate of the University of Moscow.

Where art thou coming. Springtime sweet?
  Thou com'st in vain, O Spring!
No one is left to wait for thee,
  No one thy praise to sing.

Deep darkness has enwrapped the world;
  To mount and valley cling
Red stains of blood; this year brought woe.
  Where art thou coming, Spring?

The nightingale may sing to thee;
  Who else, where all are slain,
Is left to smile? What heart can stir?
  O Spring, thou com'st in vain!

The nightingale has come, but found
  No rose with silken leaf.
Here is the flower-bed, but no flower.
  Who else is free from grief?

Although thou hast brought back the birds,
  How shall they find their nests?
No spot in all our fatherland
  Unspoiled, unruined rests.

The minstrel's mouth is closed to-day;
  No flutes or viols ring;
His heart is burning without fire.
  Where art thou coming, Spring?

No one is left to praise thee now
  On mountain or on plain;
No one is left to wait for thee;
  Spring, thou com'st in vain!

The Poet

Let your song boil with fire of ardent wrath,
  And make the soul with unfeigned sorrow ache;
Echo of noble wishes let it be,
  And sacred patriotism let it wake.

Let every note call on us to advance;
  Breathe hope to those oppressed by conflicts dread;
With immortality the fallen wreathe,
  And shame the man who like a dastard fled.

Yea, let us wrestle for the light, the truth.

Which with untruth and darkness wage their fray!
Then, bowing reverently before your face,
  "You are a poet!" we with joy will say.

Let your song ring as rings the gurgling brook
  That glides with silvery eddies mile on mile;
Let hopes and wishes bubble there like springs,
  With sounds of power, and with a vivid smile.

Make us, while we to tender voices list.
  Forget ourselves and soar to worlds above,
Where bitter tears of hardship are not shed,
  Where rest is found, and beauty glows with love.

Make us be glad and cast off grief and care,
  And live in dreams of childhood far away;
Then we shall bless the work that you have wrought;
  "You are a poet!" we with joy shall say.

Song

How often in my life to find
  Tranquillity I yearned!
Ever with visions infinite
  My heart within me burned.

The world will not afford this peace
  For which I ask in vain;
My broken, wasted heart would not
With empty hope remain.

I seek not the impossible —
  One heart to which to cling,
One feeling heart, which to its mate
  Would bring love's glowing spring.

The Incense

Madame Sybil (Zabel Klanjian Assatour) was born in Constantinople in 1863. She began very early both to write and to do benevolent work. While yet a girl, she founded one of the best organizations of women in Turkish Armenia, for the purpose of starting schools for girls in the small towns. After fifteen years of good work, the society was suppressed by the government. It was reestablished, through her efforts, after the new constitution was proclaimed in 1908. It was maintaining twenty schools when the massacres of 1915 began.
After the death of her first husband, she married Herant Assatour, a well-known literary man. Her work includes prose, poetry and translations.

Before the altar burns the fragrant incense;
  Softly the silver censer sways and bows;
The columned smoke goes up, the cross encircling.
  And with a mist anoints the saints' white brows.

Infinite sighs of prayer and of entreaty
  Under the vaults die slowly and are stilled;

Slowly the weeping flames of dim, faint ta-
pers
    Sigh, one by one, their eyes with pity filled.

Lo, a white veil, hard by the sacred column,
    Trembles with sobs that shake a hidden
frame;
In a white shadow wrapped, a heart is burn-
ing
    Silently, like the incense, in a flame.

Out of the censer's heart the incense passes,
    Winding it rises toward the ether's height.
Matter it was; the fire its life hath swallowed;
    Now 'tis but fragrance filled with colored
light.

So, too, the grieving woman's heart that
burns there
    Will not be freed from fetters and from
fires
Until it melts, dissolves, etherealizes.
    Wholly consumed by flames of pure de-
sires.

The Ideal

It is the moonlight, clear and soft, which
soon the sun outshines —
A fiery dream, which pales before the morn-
ing's stronger glow.
It is the springtime's lightning flash, a splen-
dor brief and bright;
A flower whose petals drop away when winds
awake and blow.

It is a thorny rose, which draws red blood-
drops from thine heart —
The delicate bright ribbon of the rainbow,
o'er thee hung.
It is the purple Northern Lights that play in
heaven's blue dome —
The snowy foam that scatters when against
the rock 'tis flung.

It is a feather pure and soft, blown from the
swan's white breast —
A sacred kiss beneath the sky, the open ether
deep.
That which the wind, the atmosphere, the
waters bear away
Is the Ideal — the lullaby sung to the soul
asleep.

The virgin unapproachable, by showers of
yearning sought,
The golden ring that binds us unto life, unto
the real —
The agitating multitude of dazzling youthful
dreams,
The love-song of the heart's deep void — ah,
this is the Ideal!

Tears

There are tears that fall in grief and sadness;
    Slow and mournfully the cheek they stain,
Every drop a sob, a lamentation,
    In its dew a throb of bitter pain.

There are other tears, bright, clear, untroubled,
    Shining as the sun, untouched of care,
Like the violet rain, calm, cool, refreshing.
    When the scent of earth is on the air.

There are tears all silent and mysterious.
    From the soul's love-yearning depths that steal;
They relate to us long tales of sorrow.
    Buried loves which mourning veils conceal.

There are tears that seem to me like laughter
    Like clouds tempest-tossed, that roam for aye,
Flinging lightnings to the winds of ocean,
    Drifting, mistlike, out and far away.

There's a dry tear, burning, never falling —
    Liquid flame, intense, consuming, dread —
Not to pass until the eyes are ashes.
    And the mind is ruined too and dead.

Tears, I know you all, though ye be only
    Memories of a past that sorrows fill.
Strong emotions, be ye blest forever!
    'Tis through you my heart is living still.

Murmurs of a Patriot

Mugurditch Chrimian Hairig is the grandest figure in modern Armenian history. He has been compared to Lincoln. Beginning in poverty, and possessing little education, he rose to the highest place through his native greatness of mind and heart. Born in Van in 1820, he married early, but was soon left a widower. He took holy orders, and devoted himself ardently to the cause of education, founding schools, training teachers, setting up in Van the first printing press in Armenia, publishing a magazine, and spreading enlightenment by every means. He was a strong advocate of education for girls, and in one of his books, "The Family of Paradise," he argues against the prevailing Oriental idea that husbands have a right to rub over their wives by force. All his views were progressive. His pupils went out through the country, spreading light. He protested courageously against the oppression and robbery practised on the Armenians. After the Turco-Russian war, in 1878, he was chosen a delegate, with three others, to plead the cause of the Armenians before the Congress of Berlin. His activities for his people's welfare caused him to be exiled for a time to Jerusalem. He rose from one ecclesiastical dignity to another, became Patriarch of Constantinople, and was finally elected Catholicos of all the Armenians. He was deeply loved and venerated for his wisdom and saintliness. He died in 1907, universally mourned. The affectionate surname of "Hairig" (Little Father) was given him by the people.

The following poem is dedicated "To brave Vartan and his fellow soldiers, in memory of the celebration of the Holy Martyrs." It commemorates those who fell in the battle of Avarair.

87

God-kindled soul, brave general of the host
Made strong by Christ! New Judas Macca-
beus,
Chief conqueror, giving courage for the fight,
Victorious alike in life and death!
Bold champion against the Persian faith!
For love of true religion's sacred name
And of the freedom of the fatherland,
(O greatest love!) you did not spare yourself;
You perished, and Armenia arose,

      Vartan Mamigonian!

O cross-clad warrior, spurring your white
steed,
Say, whither are you going in such haste?
The fellow soldier of brave Vartan I,
His fellow soldier of the self -same blood.
To reach the field of Ardaz forth I go;
And with the cross's arms, like butting horns,
The herds of the black goats I there shall
crush.
Go, go, your sword turned toward the ene-
my,

      Khorène Khorkhorooni!

Love-kindled soul, made wise by heavenly
lore!
Against the Persian worshipers of fire
Wisely you fought. You sacrificed yourself;
You left this world; in heaven is your reward.
Yea, with great wisdom that exchange was
made,

      Wise Humayag!

Most choice foundation rock for Ararat,
The builded of the Lord, our Mother Zion!

Broken from the top of Massis, [1] you rolled
down
To Ardaz; there you smote and you de-
stroyed
The false fire-altars of the Magian faith.
Higher the glory of the cross arose,
Satan our enemy was overcome,

      Wondrous Dajad!

Who, mounted on his black, swift-flying
steed,
With blazing eyes, looks neither left nor
right.
And goes to battle with an eager heart?
He knows that holy is the fatherland.
It is a duty high to die for it.
Go swiftly, swiftly go! I love your soul.
That vow is sacred. Give your light and life -
The light and life your country gave to you.
A death like that is immortality.
Which evil men of this world do not know,

      Ardag Balooni!

O scion of a valiant race! I love
Your stature like a plane-tree, that has raised
Your head toward heaven. 'Twas God that
made you grow.
Give, do not spare that stature, nor your life.
For church and nation; sow that ready seed.
And water it with red blood from your veins,
That it may grow into a lily fair,

      O Nerses, hero wonderfully built!

Angelic youth, graceful and beautiful.
Who came from Knooni's garden full of
flowers!

God planted you, blind Hazgerd plucked you up;
Yet living still and blooming you remain.
O what a youthful sacrifice you gave,
Of your free will, for your dear country's sake!
You, a new Sahag, nurtured tenderly,
You, of the house of good St. Gregory
Our father, like a lamb were sacrificed.
                Delicate Vahan!

Your heart full-armed with holy zeal, to take
Vengeance for faith and fatherland, the field
Of Avarair you entered, spoiled and slew
The sons of gloomy Oromisda, seeking
To light up the fire-altars, and put out
Father St. Gregory's bright-shining lamp.
Your blood put out the altars false of fire
And lighted up Armenia's burning torch.
                Amiable Arsen!

Yonder before grim Hazgerd's judgment seat,
Or here upon the field of Ardaz, aye
Forward in word, in answer, and with blade;
An ardent lover of the spotless faith
Of Jesus, and your country's liberty;
With two dear kinsmen clasped in fond embrace,
Sweetly you fell asleep. That sleep is sweet.
Let your tired arms a little while repose.
The flowers of Shavarshan, your monument.
Upon your grave, spread shade above your head,
                O forward Karekin!

Free nobles of the royal family.

Two eagles winged by love, from Osdan's hill
You, swiftly soaring, came to Avarair.
For what? Was it to hunt the unclean beasts,

The sons of Servan of the darkness born,
Tearing the flocks of sable crows to bits
With hooked claws? Bravely you fought; you smote
And you were smitten; at the last, you fell.
Nay, you are living still, and standing firm
Still, for the sake of the Armenian race,
O great Ardzrouni knights, Vahan, Sahag!

Be proud, O Gregory! Be lifted up!
Behold your lambs, who, having bravely fought
The apostate wolves, into the carnage sank.
From heaven above behold them, newly winged,
In flocks like doves, flying from earth to you!
Make broad your lap, give them a resting place;

Your sons are weary. Count them one by one.
One thousand martyrs they and thirty-six,
Whom the church sprung from you presents to heaven.

O God of Gregory, Nerses, Sahag!
God of our holy ancestors, behold
An all-devoted sacrifice for thee —
Such martyrs' sacred blood! Receive it. Lord!
Remember, Lord! Have mercy. Lord, and visit
The holy Vartan's suffering fatherland!

[1] Massis is the Armenian name of Mt. Ararat.

[2] The Persian King.

The Memorial of the Lamenting Soldier

Oh, not for me will be a grave
  With cross-marked stone to view!
I die upon the field of death;
  My name will perish too.

And not for me a splendid bier,
  Or burial's pageant vain,
Or family to mourn for me,
  Or friends for funeral train.

My tomb, which my own hands have dug,
  Will be a trench profound;
The graves of thousands of the dead
  With mine will make a mound.

Then strip me of my uniform.
  My arms and honors proud,
And leave me but my blood-stained shirt
  To serve me for a shroud.

A soldier's corpse is valued not;
  Within a trench to lie
'Tis cast, as on the threshing floor
  The sheaves are piled on high.

We from the battle-field set out,
  And we have reached our rest.
Tired soldiers of the field of blood,
  Sleep with untroubled breast!

At Gabriel's trump, our mound shall stir.
  And as in fresher guise
Eagles their plumage strong renew,
  We to new life shall rise.

Christ comes as judge, and all earth's thrones
  Before God's bar are set.
The judgment of the field of blood
  Just God will not forget.

Ye living soldiers, fare ye well!
  I leave this world. I bore
The sword, and perished by the sword,
  As Christ foretold of yore.

A farmer God created man,
  The soil to dress and till;
Curst be the hand whose wicked art
  Has taught him blood to spill!

Wise men predict a golden age
  When peace o'er earth shall breathe.
When kings shall all be reconciled,
  And swear the sword to sheathe.

The lion shall gentle grow, the wolf
  Browse by the lamb in peace,
The fields of blood with lilies bloom,
  And all earth's conflicts cease.

A dream! I do not credit it.
  Christ's words come back to me,
That nation shall 'gainst nation rise,
  Earth be a bloody sea.

O Jesus, Saviour bringing peace!

90

Our world you came and saw.
Men are insane; they have not yet
   Mastered your gospel's law.

Angel of love incarnated!
   You said all men that live
Are brethren; give to us your peace.
   Which this world cannot give!

Garine

The dismal news ran through the land of
Moush:
"Here comes the Khan Long Timour, fierce
and fell,
The despot grim who devastates the world,
And who across the earth from east to west
Has marched, and measured it with his lame
feet."

This heard the great Amira [1] of Sassoun,
And shook with fear. The crafty tyrant then
A lesson learned from Satan. He cried out,
"Oho! Oho!" His heart swelled high with
pride.
He said, "I have found out the way, the
means.

"Lo, all the people of the land of Moush
I will expel, and drive them to Sassoun;
All empty that rich country will I leave;
Nor man, nor cat, nor dog shall there re-
main.
Then when Long Timour comes into our
land.

He will behold the country desolate.
Village and town deserted of their folk;
And, struck with shame, he will turn back
again."

He spake, and gave command that it be
done.
The wild tribes of the mountains of Sassoun
Gathered like black clouds when a storm is
nigh,
They flocked together like a locust swarm,
And all came down upon the land of Moush.

Terror and panic then possessed Daron;
Moush was surrounded by a darksome fog.
The mother then disowned her infant child,
The groom forgot his bride; all tenantless
Their habitations populous they left.
And toward the vales and mountains fled
away.

Who was that heroine with a manly soul?
'Twas brave Garine of the land of Moush.
Her spouse was dead; she had an eight years'
child,
Her only and her well beloved son.

Garine was a dame of noble blood,
A scion of the house of Mamigon,
Stately and tall, in form a giantess.
Her brilliant eyes, like jewels, shone with
light;
Her face was serious and inspired respect;
Her arms were mighty, full of strength and
power.
Not crafty she, like Judith in old time;

91

She acted openly, with fearless heart.

Thinking to shun the close-impending ill,
She girt about her waist her father's sword,
Inherited from aged Mooshekh's hand;
She to her shoulder swung the shield of steel;
A brave and glorious soldier she became.
She took the little Mooshekh, her dear son,
Called on the name of God, and took the
road.

As she went forward free and fearlessly,
Lo, wicked men pursued her. Once she
turned
And strewed upon the ground that evil crew;
But in the distance when her eyes beheld
A host of brutal Koords that followed still,
She cried aloud: "Thou knowest, O my God!
I am a mother loving well my son;
But now my Christian faith and love for
Thee
Conquer the mother love within my breast.
I will forget parental tenderness,
The natural love that warms a mother's
heart,
And I to Thee will sacrifice my son.
Once Thou didst hold the arm of Abraham
Lest he should sacrifice his only son.
But do not Thou hold back mine arm,
O Lord!
Here let me sacrifice my youthful lamb."

She spoke, and drew her sword, and on the
spot
Mooshekh, her little son, she straightway
slew.

As, when we slay a fowl, it flutters wild,
So little Mooshekh at his mother's feet
Fluttered and died. The little dove's pure soul
Fled forth and joined the flock of spirits
bright.

"Oh!" then said brave Garine, "I have saved
His soul and faith. I from the Book have
learned
It is the spirit that alone gives life;
The flesh is empty, void, and nothing worth."

Thus brave Garine made her sacrifice;
And the barbarians saw the deed she did.
And they were struck with terror and amaze.
And where they stood they halted, stupefied.

But brave Garine then set forth again,
And as an eagle soars she darted up
Unto the summit of a lofty rock.
One side of it was sheer, a precipice
So deep his brain must reel who looked be-
low.

Garine there upon the rock knelt down,
And upward turned her eyes to heaven's
height,
And murmured from the bottom of her
heart:
"Ah, do not count it as a sin, my Lord!
Garine shed the blood of her young son.
Thou knowest, Lord, knowing the hearts of
all,
My sacred faith ancestral I have served
Since baptism: my virtue I have kept,

Which is Thy gift, a grace received from Thee.
Mother Shamoone I remember well —
An orphan-loving, faithful woman she.
She gave her seven sons a sacrifice,
And thus defended she her holy faith.
Thou knowest. Lord, my sacrifice is small;
Greater by far was Thine upon the cross!
Oh, give thy servant strength to sacrifice
Her life for Thee! Not from despondency
A suicide, but as a volunteer,
A victim to my love for Thee, I come!"

These were the words that brave Garine spoke.
On her bright face she signed the sacred cross,
And down that deep and dreadful precipice
She threw herself, unshrinking, to the ground.
Her body was in pieces dashed; her soul
Fled, and ascended to the heights of heaven.

The Angel oped to her the heavenly gates.
Garine entered to the realm of light,
And there she found again her little dove,
And soul was joined with soul in that bright realm;

The mother was made happy with her son.
Armenian mothers, take example hence!
Whenever you shall read these lines of mine,
The lines that agèd Hairig here has penned.
Be mindful of Garine, who, to keep
Her virtue and her pure God-given faith,
Unto destruction gave her mortal frame.

And won the heavenly kingdom by the deed.
Forever blessed be her memory!

[1] A title equivalent to Lord.

At Evening

BY BEDROS TOURIAN

Dear, I loved you when Armenia's roses
   Budded forth upon your forehead pale —
On the day those suns, your eyes, were hidden
   Bashfully behind their lashes' veil!

Freely the cool breeze your path may visit,
   And the stars gaze on you without fear.
Only I, alone amid the shadows.
   Tremble, hardly daring to draw near.

Like a breeze to-day you flee before me;
   On my lyre your shade alone you throw;
Like a comet from afar coquetting.
   While upon the air your gold locks flow.

Then the graveyard's frozen trees all whisper
   With the dead, beneath a cold wind's breath;
Then my sad heart's chords give back an echo
   To their voice, an echo calling death.

But the light sound of your footstep echoes
   Ever and forever in mine ears,
And my soul descends, with sobs and mourning,
   Into an abyss of woe and tears!

Lights and sounds have died; no leaf now
rustles;
  Mute our hearts — no breath of word or
kiss!
Kisses now and murmurs all are buried
  In the starry heavens' deep abyss.

Let the zephyr breathe upon its blossoms,
  Let the stars look down upon the sea;
Let me too grow pale, if but once only,
  When your ardent glance is cast on me!

When the crescent moon to the horizon
  Blushing sinks on yonder mountain
heights,
Then you vanish — then you walk no longer
  There before the stars, the wind, the lights.

Like a breeze that stirs the leaves and shakes
them,
  So you stirred my heart's depths, full of
fire;
And you drew from out my throbbing bosom
  Those keen cords of flame that make a
lyre.

You walk forth when day is done, my dar-
ling,
  When the starry night is cool and sweet.
Do you know how with your glance of magic
  You consume my heart beneath your feet?

To May

Virgin, mother of the sweet spring flowers!

O lovely May, in shining blossoms clad!
Why bring you not the blossom of my soul
  Among your many-colored flowerets glad?

Ah me! Another angel may there be.
  The May of the soul's flowers? Some happy
day
Then may that angel come, and on my head
  Shine with soft light — an infinite pale
May!

My Death

When Death's pale angel stands before my
face,
  With smile unfathomable, stern and chill,
And when my sorrows with my soul exhale.
  Know yet, my friends, that I am living still.

When at my head a waxen taper slim
  With its cold rays the silent room shall fill,
A taper with a face that speaks of death.
  Yet know, my friends, that I am living still.

When, with my forehead glittering with
tears,
  They in a shroud enfold me, cold and chill
As any stone, and lay me on a bier.
  Yet know, my friends, that I am living still.

When the sad bell shall toll — that bell, the
laugh
  Of cruel Death, which wakes an icy thrill -
And when my bier is slowly borne along.
  Yet know, my friends, that I am living still.

When the death-chanting priests, dark
browed, austere,
   With incense and with prayers the air shall
fill,
Rising together as they pass along,
   Yet know, my friends, that I am living still.

When they have set my tomb in order fair,
   And when, with bitter sobs and wailing
shrill,
My dear ones from the grave at length de-
part,
   Yet know, my friends, I shall be living still.

But when my grave forgotten shall remain
   In some dim nook, neglected and passed
by, -
When from the world my memory fades
away,
   That is the time when I indeed shall die!

Dawn

By Archbishop Khorene Nar Bey De Lusignan

Roses upon roses
   Spread in sheets below,
In the high blue ether
   Clouds that shine like snow,
Lightly, brightly, softly,
   Spread before thy feet,
In this tranquil season
   Wait thy face to greet;
Waits in hope all nature,
   O Aurora sweet!

Radiant, pure she rises,
   In her veil of white.
With her floating tresses
   Gleaming golden bright,
Spreading wide in ripples
   By the zephyrs swayed,
And her pearly pinions
   Opening, half displayed —
Gracious, fair Aurora,
   The celestial maid.

On her brow bright jewels
   Glow in loveliness,
And her joyous glances
   Heaven and earth caress;
While her rose-lips, brighter
   Than earth's blooming bowers,
Smiling blithely, scatter
   Perfume sweet in showers,
Making yet more fragrant
   Many-colored flowers.

Now the small birds twitter
   'Mid the leaves so green,
Blending with their rustle;
   Hail, O Dawn serene!
Hail! Thou changest darkness
   Into sunlight free.
The sad earth thou makest
   Glad and full of glee.
All created beings
   Cry "All hail!" to thee.

Unto thee each offers
   Its first gift in love,
Tenderest gift and holiest;

95

Cloud that floats above.
Zephyr, crystal streamlet,
  Flowers and nightingale —
All with love are melted,
  Praise thee, bid thee hail.
Heavenly maiden, lovely
  In thy shining veil!

Thou our hearts that charmest
  Now with such delight,
Leave us not forsaken
  In the grave's dark night!
When our eyes are closing,
  Let it beam and shine
Still before our souls' eyes,
  That sweet light of thine,
Full of hope and promise,
  Dawn, thou maid divine!

The Exile to the Swallow

O swallow, swallow, was it thine,
  This nest, all cold and drear.
That empty in this niche I found
  When first I entered here?
At sight of it mine eyes o'erflowed
  With bitter teardrops, born
Of the sad thought that my nest too
  Lies empty and forlorn.

O swallow, hasten to thy nest.
  And have no fear of me!
In me a comrade thou shalt find;
  A wanderer I, like thee.
I know the longing of thy heart.
  The yearning for thy home;

I know the bitter pains of those
  As exiles forced to roam.

Happy art thou, O bird, to find
  Thy little nest at last!
The time of thy brief pilgrimage
  Is over now and past.
Forget thy woes, chirp merrily!
  Let grief be left to me,
Who know not of my wanderings
  When there an end shall be.

Swallow, thou hadst the hope of spring,
  To reach thy home nest here;
My winter ends not; spring I lost,
  Losing my country dear.
Oh, dark to me this foreign light!
  The air is dull and dead,
Bitter the water that I drink.
  And like a stone my bread!

Swallow, when thou shalt seek again
  This nest, to thee so dear.
Wilt thou still hear my trembling voice
  Bidding thee welcome here?
If thou shalt find my humble cot
  Empty and silent stand,
Bear to my grave a drop of dew
  Brought from my fatherland!

The Armenian Girl

*M. Portoukalian was among the founders of
the Armenian patriotic movement. Born in
Constantinople about 1850, in his schooldays
he came under the influence of Chrimian,*

and he devoted himself to spreading education in Armenia. He became an editor and teacher, and organized a strong society which founded many schools. In Van, besides a Normal School for general purposes, he started a Sunday school to teach patriotism. The young people were so unwilling to study on Sunday that at first he had to pay them ten cents apiece to come; but they became so enthusiastic that many of them later gave not only their money but their lives to the cause.

The Turkish government suppressed his paper, and repeatedly closed his schools; but he had educated a generation of boys in progressive ideas. About thirty years ago he went to Marseilles, France, and started his paper, "Armenia," which he has published ever since, at the cost of much sacrifice. He organized the "Armenian Patriotic Association," which soon spread into Persia, Turkey, Europe and America. It was a great inspiration to all those Armenians who cherished revolutionary ideals, and it influenced the formation of the various revolutionary societies, the Hunchagists, Trochagists, etc. Mr. Portoukalian, however, is not an ultra radical. He has always advised against revolutionary demonstrations, foreseeing that they would lead to massacres. He felt that the first necessity was education. He has written a number of books and many political pamphlets, as well as poems and patriotic songs. For nearly half a century, he has been a devoted and self-sacrificing worker for his people.

In my country laid in ruins, where the wrecks of churches, thrones.
Grand buildings, crowns and palaces upon the ground are strewn.
You would think that their first glory they now silently lament.
A gentle maid, with face of woe, I see there, all alone.

What is this voice of mourning that she utters from her heart?
What is this flood of tear-drops from her eyes, as deep she grieves?
They wet her red cheeks, covered by her dark curls, as the dew
Of morn the rose's trembling head, all covered by its leaves.

Why so abundant are the tears outgushing from her eyes?
Lo, signs of blood (oh, terror!) upon her pupils soft!
Angels of heaven, who see those tears, have pity and descend, —
Collect them in a crystal cup and carry them aloft!

But no, not so; nay, leave them; to us those tears are pearls.
They sweeten the sad rivers whose bitter waters flow
Forth from the ruins; from each tear the gentle maiden sheds.
Amid the ruins, lilies white shall sprout, and bud, and blow.

Like the spring breeze, a perfume sweet she leaves where'er she walks.

She comes with trembling lips to kiss the ruins. Kneeling low,
With hair disheveled, arms outstretched, and tearful eyes upraised

Toward heaven, lo, lying prostrate, she laments in grief and woe.

Oh, let all the world be silent! We must hear the maid's lament.

Why mourns she thus? What sufferings are those she has to bear?
What heart but must be horror-struck to hear her trembling voice

Relate her sorrows infinite, in accents of despair?

"O God!" she cried, "how long wilt thou leave desolate this land?

How long with pangs unnumbered shall my aching heart be thrilled?
Which must I mourn — the ruins, or my brothers' shameful strife,

Who smite each other always? Oh, these days with grief are filled!

"How wretched is my nation's lot, girt round with many woes.

With snakes within and snakes without, beset on every hand!
Sons, traitors, 'gainst their mother arm; base writers who take bribes

Would teach the people conscience and the love of native land!

"God and religion, cruel ones, for you exist no more;

Your god is gold, I know full well; for it you sacrifice
All things beside, whate'er they be; but oh! from your hearts' depths

Does not one voice to torture you at any time arise?"

The Armenian Maid's Lament

When my Armenia's name I hear, my heart with violence throbs;

When all her sorrows I recall, tears flood my eyes like rain.
Was ever any country so luckless and forlorn?

With none to listen to her voice, she cries in bitter pain.

Rise, Vartan, Dikran, Aram, and your Mother once behold!

Let her laments awake you from the graves where ye abide!
And see, see how the house of Haig in exile wanders now!

'Tis banished without pity, stricken sore on every side.

Ah, Haiasdan, my mother dear, how long, alas! how long

Shall your children sigh far from you? How long must you still roam?
How long before this motherless Armenian maid shall reach

Your sacred arms, and wet with tears your tender hands, at home?

If I could fly and lay my head upon my mother's breast,
    And quench with joyful tears the flame with which my heart is rife!
Let me be once caressed by her, and greet her with a kiss,
    Then let the foeman's whetted steel there sacrifice my life!

Come, brothers and fair sisters, join hands and let us work!
    Our enemy is ignorance, look not for one elsewhere.
This foe has wrought us evil, from our mother made us part.
    We'll conquer it and drive it forth by study, love and care.

Brothers and sisters, oh, how long will you indifferent be?
    How long must we let tares be sown amid our fields of grain?
Ah, must we waken when the foe destroys and scatters all
    Unto the winds, till naught for a memorial shall remain?

Maid, let your hopeless heart be cleft, your smothered wail burst forth,
    And let it ring on every side, beneath the heaven's cope!
Yea, let it reach Armenia, and your mother, pitying, hear!

Perhaps she will console you, since in aliens is no hope.

Alas, I am afraid this pain will bring me to the grave,
    And none will echo more my voice when I "Armenia!" cry.
On every side is silence; you would think that here death reigned,
    And that, 'mid death and ruins, a lonely owl was I.

Ah, Haiasdan, to you I give my heart and soul! Accept!
    Let me die, and my Armenia arise, if this may be!
Am I imprisoned for her sake, a palace is the jail;
    And if my hands and feet are chained, that too is joy to me.

If exiled, forced by want to roam, for my Armenia's sake.
    To me shall be a paradise each place beneath the sky.
Let me but reach my aim, and then be to the gallows led;
    "Armenia!" from the gallows-tree my strangling voice shall cry.

The Imprisoned Revolutionist

Mihran Damadian was born in Constantinople about 1863. He was educated at the Armenian Catholic Seminary at Venice, Italy. He became a teacher in the Sassoun district,

and was much beloved. With H. Murad, he
led the fighting against the Turks, about the
year 1893. He was taken prisoner, and his
captors broke his leg to prevent any possibil-
ity of his escape. He was sent in chains to
Constantinople, and kept for some time in
prison. He is now living in Alexandria.

Rejoice! Another revolutionist,
  Turk, you have caught and in your prison
pent.
I too have fallen a victim to your wrath;
  But know, O tyrant, that I am content.

This is that dungeon, terrible and dark,
  To which in bonds your cruel hand, blood
red,
Brought many another like me; but of them
  Even the awful prison stood in dread.

Their hearts were dauntless and their wills of
iron,
  Their souls invincible by any foes.
You swallowed them, but straightway from
their bones
  Against you new avengers there arose.

Into this dungeon Greeks and Servians
  Entered, and divers torments they passed
through,
And Montenegrins, poor Bulgarians —
  But now with pride they all boast over you.

I kiss this rusty chain, with which you bound
  Those heroes, who defied your utmost
powers;

Whole nations have been ransomed by their
blood.
  Tremble, O tyrant! Future days are ours.

From the black clouds the lightning flashes
out;
  Even the cold flint gives forth fire; at morn
In the dark heavens the glorious sun doth
rise;
  And from his mother's pangs the child is
born.

So shall the future's joy and melody
  Come from our present sighs and tears and
pains.
Against you a whole nation shall arise,
  Roused by the clanking of our bloody
chains.

I enter prison gladly, kiss my chains.
  Embrace the darkness with its chilling
breath.
Better the gallows is than your base yoke,
  And revolutionists can sport with death.

But you, O tyrant, wherefore do you quake.
  You, brave and mighty? Are you terrified
Lest you should not forget my death? Why
fear
  When you have thrust your sword into my
side?

But no — methinks that you at last have felt
  Your persecutions will be futile all;
And that, despite your efforts, in the end

The Armenian nation will be freed from thrall.

Then what to me is prison, torture, chains?
    "Long live Armenia!" my last sigh shall be.
What care I even for death? By this my death
    The martyr nation shall at last be free!

Furfur Car (Roaring Cliff)

*Furfurcar is an overhanging mountain with
inaccessible rocky sides, around which, at the
mouth of each pass, were ranged the seven
villages that made up Dalvorig. Anyone
climbing the path from Porkh to Hosnood
hears the roaring (in local dialect furfur) of
the wind. This peculiar sound is caused by
the fierce current of the wind striking the
folds of the rocks; and from this the place
took its name.
Zovasar, Andok, Maratoog and Gepin are the
highest summits of the mountains of
Sassoun. Furfurcar is not as high, but the
passes and valleys that surround it, and the
perpendicular height of its sides, make it
almost impregnable. For many years its brave
mountaineers were able to defend themselves
successfully against all attacks. This poem
was written while they were still uncon-
quered.*

Refuge of Dalvorig's valiant men,
    Of strife and dangerous days!
Lo, all Armenia towards thee
    To-day in hope doth gaze.

Thou black and naked mountain-side,
    That, when winds o'er thee sweep,
Dost like a dragon hiss, or shore
    Wave tortured of the deep —
Thou wild and desert Roaring Cliff
    O'er Porkh that risest steep!

Many Armenian hearts, methinks,
    Till now are turned to stone;
No love or pity wakes in them
    Their brothers', sisters' moan;
But passion and fierce jealousy
    Have in them made their nest.
O that thine heights may dry our tears,
    Put heart within our breast!
O Roaring Cliff, protect the poor,
    The plundered and oppressed!

A monument of freedom,
    All glorious dost thou stand;
The ice and snow, to torrents turned,
    Lick at thy feet the sand.
Thee Zovasar and Maratoog,
    Andok and Gepin see
With envy; those far-shadowing mounts
    Are high, but thou art free.
Of our deliverance, Roaring Cliff,
    Do thou the cradle be!

Lighthouse of the Armenians thou,
    Fear of the wild Koord's heart;
Against the cruel tyrant Turk
    Our fortress-wall thou art.
Only to lions dost tliou give room,
    In den and awful cave;
Only the eagle on thy peaks

A resting place may crave.
O Roaring Cliff, be evermore
The stronghold of the brave!

If against Dalvorig countless foes
Should come, and bid us pay
Twenty years' tax, [1] "Come take it, then!"
The Armenian will say.
But, drawing to the Roaring Cliff,
He on the foe will rain
Bullets and stones, instead of gold
With interest in its train.
O wild and rocky Roaring Cliff,
Be then their shield again!

Let brave Armenians muster
From every village home,
From Berm, Karag and Khiyank,
From Khoulp and Muchtegh come;
Let Sim's heights too be populous;
Fight, o'er the precipice
Roll down the foe, that Roaring Cliff
May see a sight like this —
Koords, Turks by thousands, fallen down
Within its deep abyss!

Let Sassoun's lions assemble,
Fierce roaring, on thy crown;
Thence, like a raging torrent,
Let them toward Moush rush down.
Mowing before them briar and thorn!
Let field and town arise.
And stretch, to help Sassoun's brave men.
Their hands, with sparkling eyes.
O Roaring Cliff, give to them strength,
Courage, and high emprise!

And when Armenia shall be free,
A fortress we will rear,
Named Roaring Cliff; Armenia's flag
Shall o'er it glitter clear.
Let the surrounding valleys
And mountains joyful be!
Let the young matrons and the maids
All clap their hands for glee!
And let the cannon, that great day.
Boom out, with loud acclaim;
Let Roaring Cliff, Armenia's pride,
Be aye an honored name;
And let our land, from age to age.
Still celebrate its fame!

[1] A favorite device of oppression was to demand over again taxes that had already been paid.

The Lament of Martyred Sumpad's Mother

This poem commemorates one out of countless acts of oppression. Sumpad, a young man of Alashgerd, had just finished his studies at Erzerum, and was on his way to the village of Pakarich as a teacher in 1888. He was arrested and searched, and among his papers was found a poem one line of which read, "The Turk is as wild as a wild cedar tree." Sumpad was imprisoned and severely beaten. One morning he was found dead in his cell, the body bearing marks of poison. His mother and his sweetheart died of grief.

My dearest Sumpad, my beloved son,
  Flower of my heart and light of my sad
eyes!
The Turk hath snatched thee from my arms,
alas!
  Thou for thy nation wast a sacrifice.

"As wild as a wild cedar is the Turk,"
  Thou saidst; the enemy thy speech
o'erheard.
The more I think of it, the more I grieve;
  The wicked one took vengeance for that
word.

Hungering and thirsting for Armenian blood.
  He threw thee into prison, O my dear,
And chained thee cruelly; thy pleading pray-
ers
  The God of the Armenians did not hear.

In Erzerum's dungeon, in a corner flung,
  Long didst thou pine, and pant for air in
vain;
And when thou didst yield up thy latest
breath,
  Thou, for thy mother, couldst but clasp thy
chain.

Oh, let it reach to highest heaven, the voice
  Of my lament, a mother's sighing breath!
And let Armenia's valiant-hearted men
  Take vengeance for my son's untimely
death!

Short was thy life as that of any flower;

Soon came the sunset and the daylight's
close.
Pass thou to heaven, afar from this sad earth!
  There from thy sorrows thou shalt find
repose.

Thither will come thy sweetheart, and I too.
  To clasp each other, safe beyond earth's
strife.
I curse my fate, but bless thee, O my son,
  Since for thy country thou didst give thy
life!

The Snow

*Arshag Mahdesian, journalist and poet, was
born in Paloo. He was graduated from Eu-
phrates College at Harpoot, and took a grad-
uate course in English literature at Yale Uni-
versity. He has been actively connected with
the Armenian propaganda, has edited several
periodicals in English devoted to Armenian
topics, and at present edits in New York the
English magazine, "The New Armenia."*

The crystal dream of the deep-souled sea,
  Enthralled by the glances the blue sky
throws —
The azure fairy that bends above-
  One day on the wind's wings toward her
rose.

But now, repulsed by her changing love.
  It falls down sadly and silently.
To be crushed on earth under careless feet —
  The crystal dream of the deep-souled sea.

When it weeps its way to the sea once more.
  Forgetting sorrow and bitterness,
Toward the azure fairy again 'twill soar,
  Allured by the golden sun's caress.

Thus Spake Man

Deep sunk in thought I wandered in a city
dead by fire,
Where walls, like blackened skeletons, in
ruin rose on high.
Enshrouded by the shadow of Destruction all
things seemed.
Smothered beneath the sun that shone within
a tomb-like sky.

Destruction with its breath of flame in tri-
umph boasted high:
"Thus in one day, one moment, I destroy the
pride and grace
Of works that Man has taken years to rear
upon the earth;
And low he lies before me when I show him
my stern face!"

But Man, of mighty will power, when he
heard this haughty boast.
Raised up his sorrow-laden head, and like a
giant cried:
"Destruction, you arc longing for my down-
fall and defeat.
But you are all in error, you are blinded by
your pride.

"Creating, still creating, I shall combat you
for aye.
You may destroy, but I shall build forever-
more, with joy,
Till Godhood shall awake in me, and when
that day shall dawn
Then even grim Destruction itself I shall
destroy!"

Miscellaneous

Love Song

*Nahabed Koutchak lived in the latter part of
the 15th century. Although he wrote only
love songs, he is revered as a saint, and his
grave near Van is a place of pilgrimage.*

Thy face is like a moon that shines on earth,
  Like a thick night thy clustering tresses be;
Apples of paradise thy temples are,
  And thy deep eyes were lent thee by the
sea.

Thou hast arched brows and dark, dark eyes,
my love;
  Peerless art thou among earth's countless
girls.
Thine eyelashes are arrows to my heart;
  Thy mouth is a moist tulip, full of pearls.

104

The Lake of Van

Raffi (Hagop Melik Hagopian) was born in the village of Phayajouk in Salmast, Persia, in 1835, the son of a prominent merchant. Business reverses forced his father to take him from school and put him to work. In 1858 he traveled through Turkish Armenia, and his soul was stirred by the injustice and oppression suffered by the Armenians. In 1872, when Ardzrouni started in Tifiis his famous paper, "Mushak" (The Workman), Raffi became a regular contributor. Aroused by the terrible events of those days, he wrote for it, as serials, a number of patriotic novels — "The Fool," "Sheik Jelalleddin" and others — which thrilled the people's hearts and attained immense popularity. Some were historical novels in the style of Sir Walter Scott. He died in 1888, much regretted.

Deep silence everywhere - a hush profound!
   One might imagine nature to be dead.
Sitting here mournfully, a pilgrim lone,
   O brilliant moon, I see thee overhead.

Since the beginning of the world and time.
   Moon, thou hast run thy course. Oh, hast thou seen
The poor Armenians, once so fortunate,
   And dost thou now behold their sufferings keen?

I wonder if thou too, like me, O moon,
   Seeing Armenia 'neath barbarian feet,
Dost shed salt tears of grief and bitterness,
   And in thy heart do piercing arrows meet?

Thy heart is like a rock, thy conscience dead.
   How many massacres have met thine eye,
How many a carnage! yet thou buildest now
   Again a bright arch o'er Armenia's sky.

Wherefore this silence? Speak to me, O lake!
   Wilt thou not weep with me, whose heart is rent?
O breezes, stir the waves to billows high.
   And with these waters let my tears be blent!

From the beginning all things thou hast seen
   That in Armenia happened. Tell us, pray,
Whether Armenia, once a garden fair,
   Shall always be a thorny desert gray?

Oh, can it be, our nation, full of woe.
   Shall 'neath a foreign prince's sway lie prone?
Oh, can it be, the Armenians and their sons
   Are found unworthy before God's high throne?

Will a day come when from Mt. Ararat
   A banner shall be seen, by breezes fanned.
And when Armenian pilgrims everywhere
   Shall start for their beloved fatherland?

'Tis hard, O Heavenly Ruler! but inspire
   Their souls, and let Thy light of knowledge flame
O'er them, to show them what is human life -

They by their works shall glorify Thy name!

Upon the lake there shone a sudden light;
  A graceful maid rose from the waters there;
A lighted lantern in one hand she bore,
  In one a shining lyre of ivory fair.

Was she some nymph, some peerless angel? Nay,
  A matchless fair Armenian Muse was she.
Muse, read the fate of the Armenians!
  The present and the future tell to me!

That sweet celestial spirit spoke: "Good news
  I bring to thee, young pilgrim! Dry thine eyes.
New, happy days shall come; when reigns God's will
  Freely, the Golden Age again shall rise.

"Armenia's Muses will awake again,
  And her Parnassus blossom gloriously;
The car of Phoebus, shedding light abroad,
  Shall circle round Armenia's gloomy sky.

"We too, like thee, passed many mournful days.
  When a dark night, that seemed it ne'er would cease,
Enwrapped Armenia; and we too, dear youth,
  Have now received the olive branch of peace.

"Wipe thy lyre's rusted strings with joy to-day,

Go to Armenia with an ardent song!
Awake the zeal of the Armenians,
  Their zeal benumbed in lethargy so long.

"The time has come, the time so long desired;
  Fulfilled is now the old prophetic word;
The day will dawn; behold the morning star,
  A sign made visible — thus saith the Lord!"

Then darkness fell, the figure disappeared;
  But long was heard the voice of sweetness rare,
Mixed with the murmur of the lapping waves,
  And aromatic fragrance filled the air.

O happy news! O tidings glad and sweet!
  What joy, fair Muse, for sad and sorrowing men!
Tell us, reveal if it be possible
  For a dead corpse to wake and live again!

The Eagle's Love

Shoushanik Kourghinian was born at Alexandropol in 1876. She soon became known through her contributions to the press. Her first volume of collected poems, "The Tolling Bells at Dawn," appeared in 1907. Most of them are poems of freedom and of the labor movement. She has had little schooling, but has educated herself.

The eagle sat upon the rocky verge;
He sat and sang — the wild notes filled the
air.
He saw the maiden in the vale below;
He marked how beautiful she was, how
fair.

"Good girl, thou maiden like the reindeer
fleet!
How sad it is thou hast not learned to fly!
In silence, in that place of shadow deep,
Thou like a flower wilt fade away and die.

"O lovely maid, if thou couldst only fly.
Queen would I make thee of my rocky
steep!
And if thine eyes grew heavy, on my wings
I with sweet songs would cradle thee to
sleep.

"To me those eyes of thine are darksome
night,
Thy smile a burning sun, like that above.
The heaven vast would not rule over thee,
But would become thy vassal, for thy love.

"I wonder if thou canst not fly at all?
Who gave thee birth, devoid of wings for
flight?
I wonder if thou never in thy life
Hast longed to soar in air, all free and
light?"

Thus the proud eagle from the rocky verge
Sang, longing for the maiden for his mate.
He flew away, and soared o'er hills and vales,

Mourning and grieving for the maiden's
fate.

Fatherland

*Avedik Issahakian was born in Alexandropol
in 1875. He received part of his education in
Germany. He began to write in 1891. His
collected poems, "Songs and Wounds," ap-
peared in 1903.*

HE, my fatherland, how lovely thou art.
Thy mountain peaks are lost in the mists of
heaven.
Thy waters are sweet, thy breezes are sweet;
Only thy children are in seas of blood.
May I die for thy soil, thou priceless father-
land!
Oh, it is little if I die with one life!
Would that I had a thousand and one lives
To offer thee, all from my heart.
To die for thy sorrow with a thousand lives!
Let me offer myself for thy children, for love
of thee!
Let me keep for myself only one life.
That I may sing the praise of thy glory.
That I may soar high like the skylark
On the rising of thy new day, noble father-
land,
And sing sweetly, praise loudly
Thy bright sun, thou free fatherland!

107

The Sure Hope

By Raphael Patkanian

Let the wind blow cold, let it beat my face,
Let the clouds above heavy snowflakes fling,
Let the north wind blow, raging all it will, —
Yet I live in hope soon or late comes spring.

Let the heavy clouds make the clear sky dark,
Let the dense fogs cover the earth from sight,
Let the elements be together mixed,
Yet I know the sun will again be bright.

Let harsh trials come, persecutions rage.
And the light grow dim of the sun on high;
To Armenian hearts, pain is naught to dread -
But the poor man's hope must not fade and
die!

The Lullaby of Nazi

*Avedis Aharonian, born at Igtir, Erivan, in
1866, has written novels, short stories, liter-
ary criticisms, dramas and poems. At the
time of Abdul Hamid's massacres, he was
living near the frontier between Turkey and
Russia, and he saw the sufferings of the refu-
gees, and took part in the relief work. His
graphic tales, called out by these events,
made a deep impression. While in the Cau-
casus a few years ago, he was imprisoned by
the Russian government as a political offend-
er, and he came out with broken health. His
writings are highly esteemed.*

Oh, sleep, my little one; oh, sleep once more!
  Thou need'st not weep, for I have wept full
sore.

The blind wild geese flew, screaming mourn-
fully,
  Across our heavens black, o'er vale and
hill.
Blinded they were among our mountains
high!
  Thou need'st not weep, for I have wept my
fill.

The gale is moaning in the forests dark;
  'Tis the lament of homeless corpses chill.
Ah, many and many a corpse unburied lies!
  Thou need'st not weep, for I have wept my
fill.

Laden with tears, the caravan passed by,
  Knelt in the forest black, and stays there
still.
It was our land's calamities and woes!
Thou need'st not weep, for I have wept my
fill.

Beads have I strung and on thy cradle bound,
  To guard thee from the foeman's evil eye.
Oh, sleep and grow, my little one, make
haste!
  Thou need'st not weep; my tears were sel-
dom dry.

My milk has frozen on thy pallid lips;
  'Tis bitter, and thou dost not want it more;

108

With it is mixed the poison of my grief.
   Thou need'st not weep, for I have wept full sore.

Oh, with my milk drink in my black grief too!
Let it black vengeance in thy soul instill!
Shoot up, my darling, grow to stature tall!
Thou need'st not weep, for I have wept my fill.

The Martyrs of Avarair

By Bishop Karekin Servantzdiantz

If Coghtn's patriot bards are silent now,
   Whose songs of old wreathed heroes with renown,
Then let immortal spirits come from heaven.
   Let them descend, Armenia's brave to crown.

Let flocks of angels come from heaven, and sit
   On Ararat's high top, where cloud-wreaths brood.
God has descended unto Haiasdan
   To scent the savor of Armenian blood.

O clouds, fly far away from Shavarshan!
   Shed there no more your dews through darkening air,
For Shavarshan is watered by the blood
   Of the Armenian brave who perished there.

No grass, no rose springs up or blossoms there
   Upon that field which is our heroes' tomb;
But where the mighty Vartan fell and died.
   The flower of sacred faith shall bud and bloom.

Brave Egiché, the sculptor, to Ardaz
   Comes with his pen in hand, and fair and straight
He cuts and measures, he inscribes and stamps
   The valiant Vartan's life and death and fate.

O Ararat, raise monasteries, shrines,
   Domes cross surmounted, temples fair to see,
Gospel and cross, a lasting monument
   That worthy of great Vartan's name shall be!

Shine on the mountain chain of Kaght, O sun!
   In its dark niches let your beams arise.
'T was there brave Humayag in battle fell,
   'T is there that he, a holy martyr, lies.

Moon, o'er the bones of the Armenians
   Watch with your wakeful eye from heaven's blue deep,
And with the happy dews of smiling May
   Sprinkle the lonely graves wherein they sleep!

Eagles and falcons of Armenia,
 And cranes, her summer guests from age
to age,
Over this land keep watch, and let the house
 Of the Armenians be your heritage!

Perch on the ashes; in the ruins old,
 Armenian birds, make ye your nests, your
home,
And let the flitting swallow come and go,
 Until for the Armenians spring shall come!

The Waves on the Shore

*Bedros Adamian, a famous Armenian actor,
was born in 1849, and died in 1891. He
wrote many poems and translations.*

The day is bright June weather,
 The cool north wind blows free;
Why swells thy breast, old ocean?
 Hast thou good news for me?
Thy billows, coming, coming,
 Leap high, then sink away,
And on the shore forever
 Scatter their foaming spray.

O billows, ocean billows,
 These rocks and sands that fret!
Bring tidings of the dear ones
 My heart can ne'er forget!
Coming and ever coming,
 And breaking o'er and o'er,
Bring some glad news to cheer me,
 A pilgrim on this shore.

Consumed by mournful yearning,
 Far distant from my sight,
E'en now my dearest suffers.
 She sorrows day and night.
Her tears are ever flowing,
 Her sad heart full of care;
O billows of the ocean,
 To her my greeting bear!

Open, ye waves, and swallow
 The salt tears from mine eyes,
And bury in your bosom
 My grief, my bitter sighs!
O billows, now receding
 Back toward the ocean blue,
Receive me as your comrade
 And let me go with you!

Take me, O waves, and cast me
 Like wreckage at their feet,
A witness to the love and grief
 That bid my sad heart beat!
O billows, ocean billows.
 Waves of the great salt sea,
Come, bear me to my dear ones;
 Your comrade I will be!

The Dying Poet

By Tigrane Yergate

Why should not I, like the great poet, wear
Laurels upon my hair?
And why around my heart, for my relief,
Should they not ring, those songs deep sor-
rows sing,

110

Which from the heart like some dark essence spring.
　Making the mourning great as is the grief?

When fate oppresses me and lays me low.
Why should I yield to woe,
　Nor lift my brow with curses on my breath?
Grief can like wine intoxicate, in truth.
And grief can sing your glory and your youth,
　Then lay you low in death!

What matter that at twenty years you die
　If fame immortal shall your memory crown.
　And o'er your bier the Angel of Renown
Exalt you to the sky?

Would you, a frail old man, drag out your days
　Amid the foolish throng.
And let them mock you as your life decays.
　While for your goods they long?

Come, dream no longer! Take your harp and sing.
　When on our lakes a bird falls nigh to death,
Far rings his voice, more touching is his note;
　The tall reeds shiver with a sighing breath.

He spreads his wings in a last flight, and looks
　At the far heights — his song with sorrow rife —

And then falls, shattered at his high cliff's foot.
　Naught has he carried with him out of life;

Yet a vague memory of boundless grief
　Shall linger long upon the shore, the waves,
Like magic sweetness of a broken lute.
　Or sound of teardrops falling upon graves.

Sing, poet, sing to-day your latest hymn!
　In your endeavor. Glory smiles on you.
Poet, remember, to the world you speak,
　And you in dying shall be born anew!

The Bouquet

By Khorene M. Antreassian

Twilight's last ray is fading from the world;
　Hushed are the varied sounds of grief and mirth;
And, like a jealous consort, exiled Night
　Is now returning to embrace the earth.

Sitting beside the open window here.
　Mine eyes are fixed upon the sweet bouquet
Whose myriad petals silently repose,
　Leaning fair head to head, in loving way.

Thou art not mine, thou beautiful bouquet,
　That seemest mystic sentiments to teach;
Unknown to me the hand that gathered here
　These flowers, which once were strangers each to each.

Yet over me a nameless sadness steals.
  As, dreaming silently, I gaze on thee;
And in my stormy heart old thoughts awake,
  And many a sweet, soul-moving memory.

Thou hast a secret that I cannot pierce.
  Perchance an ardent message from some
heart
Thou hidest deep among thy petals fair;
  Interpreter of silent thoughts thou art.

With thy rich hues, so stainless and so
bright,
  Thou stirrest my sad soul victoriously.
Full many a long and dreary year has passed
  Since any friend bestowed a flower on me.

Not for this only, on this foreign shore,
  Thou movest me with memories of the
past;
Thou dost evoke a question from my heart -
  A question sorrowful, profound and vast.

These flowers of many hues bloomed far
apart,
  And each unknown to each, until this day;
Yet with what ease they here unite to form
  A lovely and harmonious bouquet!

A hand, a gentle hand, collected them.
  And now without complaint, without a
care,
They wait their fate together, lip to lip,
  Till the last sleep shall overtake them there.

Ah, why from this world's garden great and
wide.
  When human flowers together meet and
stay —
Flowers differing in fragrance, form and hue
  Seldom can they unite in a bouquet?

Unhappy Days

By Djivan

The mournful and unhappy days, like winter,
come and go.
  We should not be discouraged, they will
end, they come and go.
Our bitter griefs and sorrows do not tarry
with us long;
  Like customers arrayed in line, they come,
and then they go.

Over the heads of nations persecutions, trou-
bles, woes.
  Pass, like the caravan along the road; they
come and go.
The world is like a garden, and men are like
the flowers;
  How many roses, violets and balsams come
and go!

Let not the strong then boast themselves, nor
let the weak be sad.
  For divers persons of all kinds pass on,
they come and go-
Fearless and unafraid the sun sends forth his
beaming light;
  The dark clouds toward the house of pray-
er float past, they come and go.

112

Earth to her well-taught son belongs, with motherly caress,

But the unlettered races like nomads come and go.
Djivan, a guest-room is the world, the nations are the guests;

Such is the law of nature; they pass — they come and go.

The Prisoner to the Swallow

O strayed and wandering swallow, little bird,
    How sadly by my prison dost thou sing!
Dost thou lament because thy lovely mate
    Has left thee, and naught else can comfort bring?

Grieve, then, like me! Yet thou art fortunate,
    Thrice fortunate, for thou canst fly afar,
Flit through the valleys and across the hills
    On thy swift wings, unstayed by bolt or bar.

But here the sun itself with pallid ray
    To my dark prison cannot penetrate;
No gentle breeze blows here to bear my voice
    Unto my dear ones, telling of my fate.

At least thou goest to find my well beloved.
    Oh, swiftly dart! But then return once more
Near me, the wretched one, and tarry here,
    O swallow, tarry till this night be o'er.

Stay here to-night and witness my sad death.

And, twittering o'er my grave with dew-drops wet,
Do thou, at least, O bird, remember me —
    Remember me, and mourn, and ne'er forget!

Homesickness

I was a quince-bush growing on a rock.
    A rocky cliff that rose above the dell;
They have uprooted and transplanted me
    Unto a stranger's orchard, there to dwell;

And in this orchard they have watered me
    With sugar-water, that full sweetly flows.
O brothers, bear me back to my own soil.
    And water me with water of the snows!

The Prisoner's Dream

I am a bird, a small wild bird,
    In freedom wont to dwell;
But men have caught and caged me up
    Within this narrow cell.

From my companions parted now,
    My heart is sad and sore
Because I mingle with the flock
    No more, alas! no more.

If they should bring to sing to me,
    Here where I pine apart.
The nightingale and turtledove,
    It would not cheer my heart;

Nor if they brought me as a gift
    A thousand feathers fair
Of every hue, nor richest wine.
    Nor candies sweet and rare;

Nor if they gave me power to sway
    Vast kingdoms at my word,
Or made me of a myriad men
    The master and the lord;

Or gave me servants in a crowd,
    And countless horsemen bold,
Or built for me a palace fair,
    Adorned with gems and gold.

But could I from this cell escape
    In which my life they lock.
And fly away, and soar toward heaven,
    And see again my flock,

And mingle with it, sporting wild,
    Singing with gladsome voice,
My heart, that aches with loneliness,
    Would 'mid the flock rejoice.

The Mother Is Like Bread

The mother is like warm bread; he who eats of it feels satisfied.
The father is like pure wine; he who drinks of it feels intoxicated.
The brother is like the sun, which lights up the mountains and the valleys.

Parting Song

Sung as the bride leaves her home.

The Chorus:

The evening wind has risen,
The chief men have gathered.
May I be a sacrifice for thy soul which goes into exile!
The strings of the purse have been unloosed,
The daughter has been parted from her mother.
The avalanche is coming down from Dilif,
It is carrying away our little moon!
The foot is in the stirrup;
The mother weeps to see her go.

The Bride:

I do not want to go, mamma! I do not want to go!
They are taking me by force!
Do thou, little mother, wish that it may bring me good luck,
The milk that thou hast given me, that it may bring me good fortune!
Do thou, little father, wish that it may bring me good luck,
The bread that thou hast earned for me, that it may bring me good fortune!
Do not groan, threshold of my home;
It is for me to groan.
Do not creep, O sun!
It is for me to creep.
Do not shake, little tree!
It is for me to shake.

114

Do not fall, O leaf!
It is for me to fall.
Do not shine, O star!
It is for me to shine.
Do not rise, O moon!
It is for me to rise.
Do not weep, mamma!
It is for me to weep-

The Wanderer

Oh, heavy hearted is the wanderer
  In foreign lands, who hath his country left!
In gazing on the fever of his heart,
  Even the rocks with sorrow would be cleft.

When you on any man would call a curse,
  Say, "Be a wanderer from your native land!
And may your pillow be the mountain side,
  And may you sleep at night upon the sand!

"And, when you think upon your fatherland,
  May you from head to foot be full of
pains!"
My heart is a cracked vase; in vain I pour
  Water therein; unfilled it still remains.

Each bird of heaven hath its companion
found,
  I am alone and solitary still;
Each stone is fixed and quiet in its place;
  I roll forevermore by vale and hill.

The Mother's Lament

Look and weep, I, this child's mother. I say, "Alas for me! What will become of me now, unhappy that I am? I have seen my golden son dead!"

The fragrant rose has been snatched from my bosom; my soul faints within me! My beautiful golden dove has been made to take flight from my arms; my heart is broken!

My pretty, softly-cooing turtle-dove, death's falcon has struck it, and has wounded me. My sweet-voiced little lark has been taken from me and carried away to heaven.

My verdant pomegranate tree, all covered with flowers, the hailstorm has destroyed it before mine eyes — the reddening apple upon my tree, the fragrant fruit among my leaves!

My beautiful almond tree all in blossom, they have shaken it and left it without a fruit; they have seized it and thrown it to earth, and trampled the ground where it lies.

Oh, what will become of me, unhappy that I am! Many griefs have come upon me. At least, O God, receive the soul of my child, and let it rest in thy bright heaven!

The Dead Wife to Her Husband

I am going to turn into an eagle. I shall go and perch before thy window; I shall lament so bitterly that sleep will flee away from thee forever. Anyone else may sleep; but thou and I, henceforth, shall know sleep no more!

The Sister's Lament

The brother is the artery of his sister's heart. He has only to speak one gentle word to make her happy.

Come, my brother! Come, water of my fountain!
I am athirst for thee; whither hast thou gone?
Thou hast left me in the shadow; make light spring forth!
The wall of my love has crumbled; come and rebuild it!

Song of the Emigrant's Wife

The road on which my absent husband passes, I wish I were that road! The water-course where he goes to drink, I wish I were the spring of that water! He would have stooped to drink of that water, and the wish of my heart would be fulfilled.

In the city where he alights, I wish I were the inn-keeper, so that he would come and alight at my inn! I would take him to my best room, I would twine my arms about his neck, and talk with him sweetly.

The Orphan's Lullaby

SAHAG is on the mountain,
  Thy father 'neath the stone;
The reeds thy cradle are, thy roof
  The arching rock alone.

Oh, may the south wind rock thee,
  Beneath the midnight sky,
And may the little stars of heaven
  Sing thee a lullaby!

And may the wild ewe nourish thee
  Upon her milk so white.
That thou may'st bud, that thou may'st bloom.
  And grow in strength and height!

Oh, hushaby, my darling!
  Lilies on thy pink face!
Sleep, child, and may the wind that sings
  Blow o'er thy cradle-place!

Oh, may the wild ewe suckle thee.
  And be thy nurse the sun!
May the moon sing thy cradle song!
  Sleep, sleep, my little one!

A Knock at the Door

The wind that from the lofty summits blew
  Knocked at the door; the young wife rose and ran,
In haste, with eager steps and beating heart,
  To fling it wide. Alas, 'twas not her man!

With breaking heart she to the hearth re-
turned.

Her husband's mother spoke, to comfort
fain:
"Daughter-in-law, my little daughter, say.

Why dost thou weep? Tell me, where lies
thy pain?"

"Mother, my little mother! Everywhere
I am in pain, so for thy son I yearn."
"Weep not, my little daughter! To my son
A letter I will write, and say, 'Return'!"

"If to thy son thou writest to return,
May'st thou enjoy the light of God's bright
throne!
But, if thou dost not write him to return,
Receive my curse, and turn into a stone!"

The Song of the Goat

The goat went to play on the ice. She fell and
broke her foot. She said: "Ice, then you are
very strong?"

"If I were very strong," said the ice, "the
sun would not have thawed me."

She went to the sun and said, "Sun, then
you are very strong?"

"If I were very strong," said the sun, "the
cloud would not have covered me."

"Cloud," said she, "then you are very
strong?"

"If I were very strong, the wind would not
have scattered me."

"Wind," she said, "then you are very
strong?"

"If I were very strong, I should not have
been able to glide through the chink in the
wall."

"Chink in the wall, then you are very
strong?"

"If I were very strong, the mouse would
not have reigned over me."

"Mouse," she said, "then you are very
strong?"

"If I were very strong, the cat would not
have caught me."

"Cat," said she, "then you are very
strong?"

The cat said, shaking his tail, "I am strong,
I am strong, I am the chief of the strong! I
am the fur of great lords; I am the head-dress
of great ladies. In the village in summer, and
by the fireside in winter, I sleep a sweet
sleep. If anyone says, 'Scat!' I scud away, I go
and sit in the top of a tree."

The Dark Damsels

A spring on Mount Menzour flows out under
the long-haired willow tree. Two beautiful
dark damsels have come to fill their pitchers.
Two young men, as strong as athletes, are
passing by on horseback.

"Young girl, by the youth of thy brother,
give me a drop of water from thy pitcher!"

"The water in my pitcher is not cold, it is
hot. More men than one have died because
they loved us."

117

"Pour me a drop, let me drink, and let me die also, and let it be with me as if my mother had never given me birth!"

Playmates

Baby, in your little bed
  How beautiful you are!
Whom shall I bring to play with you,
  Searching both near and far?
For playmates I will bring to you
  The moon and morning star!

Cradle Song

The nightingale, for love of the rose, cannot sleep the whole night long. He cannot sleep during the night, nor during the day until the evening. Go to bed, and sleep sweetly, until the morning light comes, until the good light comes! Then my nightingale will wake again, my nightingale will wake again, with eyes half open and half closed.

Lullaby

Sing the cradle song so that when you hear it, you may lie down and fall sweetly asleep. Go to sleep, my child, and grow — grow and become a great man; spread out and become a village! In the village where there is no great man, become the great man of that village. Become a great forest, burying your roots deep in the earth; plunge your roots down into the very depths of the earth, and may your trees with their branches cast their shadow everywhere!

Hushaby

Hushaby, hushaby! The does have come. They have come, the does, they have come down from the mountains. They have brought thee sweet sleep, they have poured it into thine eyes, as large as seas; they have put thee to sleep with a sweet slumber; they have satisfied thee with their sweet milk.

Hushaby, hushaby! May the Lord give thee sleep! May Mother Mary grant thee peace; may Mother Mary grant thee peace so that thou mayest lie down and fall softly asleep! Of Mother Mary we will make thy mother, and of her only son thy protector. I will go to church to beg the saints to pay for us. Of the holy crucifix I will make a brother, that it may keep its arms stretched out over us forever.

Sad Snow

What art thou, O thou light and fleecy snow?
  A flower, a coverlet, a winding sheet?
That o'er Armenia's plains thou spreadest far,
  Unfolded white and wide, the sky to meet?

Or art thou a white dove from Paradise,
  That, when it saw the Holy Virgin there.
Shook down the snowy feathers from its wings
  To form a scarf upon her shoulders bare?

Or cam'st thou from the angels up above,
  Who sometimes seek their future fate to know,
Playing on high, "To die or not to die?" [1]
  With roses white, whose petals drift below?

Or art thou downy cotton or soft wool
  That the north wind upon Armenia sheds,
A pure and restful pillow to become
  Beneath our martyred sires' and brothers' heads?

If 'tis a feathery scarf thou art, snow!
  Be swaddling bands and cradle soft as silk
To children small who perished at their birth,
  Ere they had tasted of their mothers' milk!

If thou art rose-leaves, pure and stainless snow,
  Oh, then bud forth, a fresh and dewy wreath,

Upon the lowly and forsaken mounds
  Where slim Armenian maidens sleep in death!

O mournful snow, fall thick and heavily
  And cover mount and valley, rock and plain!
Cover the graves, that through the days to come
  Unbroken their sweet slumber may remain!

Those martyrs for their nation and the cross,
  Now and forever, silent and alone.
In hope of immortality in heaven,
  Repose in death, with no memorial stone.

[1] The Armenians play, "To die or not to die?" with flower petals as we play, "He loves me, he loves me not."

Appendix

The Armenian Women

The following extract from an Armenian classic will give some idea of the poetical prose of the Armenians. Eghiche, an Armenian bishop and historian of the fifth century, writing nine hundred years before Chaucer, gives a graphic account of the Persian invasion of 451 A.D., of which he was an eye-witness. In the eighth chapter he speaks as follows of the fortitude shown b} the Armenian women after the princes and nobles had been killed or carried away into captivity, and the country reduced almost to a desert: —

"But I cannot enumerate all the wives of the heroes, both of those who were in fetters, and those who had fallen in battle; for there are more whom I do not know than those whom I know. I know by name and by sight about five hundred; not only those who were the highest in rank, but many of low degree. All of them together, being kindled by a holy emulation, put on the same virtue of fidelity. They forgot even the name of the luxury belonging to their hereditary freedom, and became like men who have suffered from the beginning after the manner of peasants, and who have passed their lives in this world amid hardships. The elder ones took upon themselves the greater endurance. They were comforted by the invisible force of the eternal hope, and accepted the heavy burden of bodily pain. For although each of them had had hereditary servants, there was now nothing to distinguish between mistress and maid. All wore the same dress, and all alike slept on the ground. Neither one made the other's bed. There was no distinction even in their food. All the mattresses were of the same dark color, and all the pillows were alike black. They had no special makers of spiced dishes, nor bread-makers set apart for service at table, but everything was in common. None poured water on the other's hands, neither did the younger ones offer towels to the elder. The delicate women had no soap, nor was oil offered to them for rejoicing. No costly platter was set before them, neither were cup-holders found at their festivals. For none of them did an usher stand at the door, neither were the nobles called by them.

"The bridal chambers of the young brides became dusty and dim, and spiders' webs were spun in their sleeping-rooms. The high seats of their palaces were destroyed, and the vessels of their table service were in disorder. Their palaces fell, and the fortresses of their refuge crashed down in ruin; their flower-gardens dried up and withered, and the wine-bearing vines of their vineyards were torn up. With their eyes they saw the spoiling of their goods, and with their ears they heard of the sufferings of their dear ones. Their treasures were confiscated, and nothing at all was left of the ornaments of their faces.

"The delicately reared women of the land of Armenia, who had been brought up in luxury and petted in costly clothing and on soft couches, went untiringly to the houses of prayer, on foot and bare-footed, asking with vows that they might be enabled to endure their great affliction. Those who from childhood had been reared on oxen's brains and the choicest pieces of deer, now were glad to eat vegetable food, like savages. The skins of their bodies, blackening, became dark, because by day they were sun-burned, and all night they slept on the ground. The everlasting psalms were the murmurs of their lips, and their complete comfort was in the reading of the prophets.

"The women paired off two by two, like the animals, as equal and harmonious, drawing straight the furrow of the kingdom, that they might reach the harbor of peace without fail. They forgot their womanly weakness, and became brave males in the spiritual warfare. Doing battle, they fought against the cardinal sins; they pulled up and threw away their deadly roots. With simplicity they conquered guilefulness, and with sacred love they washed away the dark coloring of envy. They cut off the roots of avarice, and the death-bearing fruits of its branches dried up. With humility they trampled upon arrogance, and with the same humility they reached the heavenly height. With prayers they opened the closed doors of heaven, and with holy petitions caused the angels of redemption to descend. They heard the good tidings from afar, and glorified God in the highest.

"The widows among them became again as virtuous brides, and put away from them the reproach of widowhood. And the wives of those who were in fetters willingly restrained the physical appetites, and became partakers of the sufferings of the imprisoned saints. In their lives they resembled the brave martyrs in their deaths, and from a distance they became teachers of consolation to the prisoners. With their fingers they worked and were fed, and the pensions granted them by the court they sent year by year to their husbands, for their comfort. They became like the bloodless cricket, which lives without food, by the sweetness of its song.

"The snows of many winters melted, the spring arrived, the new birds came, life-loving men saw and rejoiced; but they could never see those for whom they longed. The spring flowers reminded them of their loving husbands, and their eyes longed in vain to see the desirable beauty of their faces. Their hounds died, and their hunting excursions were ended. No yearly festivals brought them from afar. The women looked on their dining-places and wept; and they remembered them in all their assemblies. Many monuments were raided to them, and the names of each inscribed thereon.

"But while thus upon all sides their minds were storm-beaten, the women did not retreat, nor weaken in heavenly virtue. To outsiders they appeared mourning and sorrowful widows, but in their own souls they were adorned with heavenly love. They ceased to ask any one who had come from a distance, "When shall we see our dear ones?" The desires of their prayers to God were only that they might finish their course with courage, filled with heavenly love, even as they had begun.

"And may we and they inherit together the Mother City of goodness (the heavenly Jerusalem) and those things which are promised to the beloved of God in Christ Jesus Our Lord! Amen."

The Armenian Church

The Armenian Church may be roughly described as about half way between the Greek Church and High Church Episcopalianism. Its head, called the Catholicos, has his see in a very ancient monastery at Etchmiadzin in Russian Armenia, near the foot of Mt. Ararat.

Under the preaching of missionaries, a part of the Armenians have become Protestants, and another part Roman Catholics; but the great bulk of them still adhere to their ancient national church.

The Armenians are eager for education, and have flocked in large numbers to the many schools and colleges that have been maintained in Asia Minor for years by the American Board of Foreign Missions, until the massacres and deportations of 1915-16 deprived them of almost all their pupils.

Owing to centuries of persecution, Armenian colonies are scattered all over the world. There are said to be fully 250,000 Armenians in the United States, and some estimates place the number much higher.

Bibliography

Persons who wish to look into Armenian history, literature, folklore, etc., will find the following works of interest:

"Armenia: Travels and Studies," by Henry F. B. Lynch, London, Longmans, Green Co., 1901; "Armenia and Europe," by J. Lepsius, London, 1897; "Armenia and the Armenians,"' by E. J. Dillon (a section in his "Russian Characteristics"); "Historical Sketches of Armenia and the Armenians in Ancient and Modern Time," with special reference to the present crisis, by an old Indian, London, 1896; "Turkish Armenia and Eastern Asia Minor," by H. F. Tozer, London, 1881; "Twenty Years of the Armenian Question," by James Bryce in his "Transcaucasia and Ararat," pages 446-525, 1896; "Travel and Politics in Armenia," with an Introduction by Viscount Bryce, and a contribution on

Armenian history and culture by Aram Raffi, by Noel Edward Buxton and Harold Jocelyn Buxton, London, Smith, Elder & Co., 1914; "Through Armenia on Horseback," by George H. Hepworth, New York, Dulton & Co., 1898; "Travels in Armenia," by A. H. Layard, London, 1853; "The Armenian Church — History, Liturgy, Doctrines, and Ceremonies," by Edward Francis For- lcscue, London, J. T. Hayes, 1872; "The Rule of the Turk," by Frederick D. Greene, New York, Putnam, 1896; "Turkey and the Armenian Atrocities," by E. M. Bliss; "Travels and Researches in Mesopotamia and Armenia," by W. F. Ainsworth, London, 1842; "Armenia and the Armenians," by R. D. James Is- saverdens, Venice, 1878; "Researches in Armenia," by F. Smith, Boston, 1833; "Impressions of Turkey during Twelve Years' Wandering," by W. M. Ramsay, New York, Putnam, 1897; "England's Responsibility toward Armenia," by Malcolm MacColl, London, Longmans, 1895; "Armenian Women, Their Folk Poesy," by L. M. J. Garnet in her "Women of Turkey," pages 270-296; "Arme- nians, Kurds and Turks," by J. Creagh; "Life and Adventures in Trebizond, Erzerum, Tabriz," by A. Vambery, London, 1886; "Armenia and the Campaign of 1877," by C. B. Norman, London, 1878; "The Armenian Campaign," by C. Williams, London, 1878; "The Armenians, or the People of Ararat," by M. C. Gabrielian, Philadelphia, Allen, Lane & Scott, 1892; "The Leavening of the Levant," by Joseph K. Greene, Revell Press, 1916; "The Golden Maiden and Other Folk and Fairy Tales Told in Armenia," by A. G. Seklemian, with Intro- duction by Alice Stone Black well, Cleveland, O., Helman Taylor Co., 1898; "Armenian Mythology," compiled by Zabel S. Boyajian, London, G. M. Dent & Sons, 1916; "The Blackest Page of Modern History," by Herbert Adams Gib- bons, New York, Putnam, 1916.

In French: "Contes Arméniens, Traduits de l'Armenien Moderne," by Frédé- ric Macler, Leroux, Paris, 1905; "Mekhitaristes de Saint Lazare, Histoire d'Arménie, Littérature Arménienne," by Paul Emile Le Vaillant de Florival, Venice, Typographie Arménienne de Saint Lazare; "L'Arménie Chrétienne et sa Litterature," by Felix Neve, C. Peters, Louvain, 1886; "L'Armenie; son His- toire, sa Littérature, son Rôle en L'Orient, avec une Introduction par Anatole France," by Archag Tchobanian, Paris, Société du Mercure de France, 1897; "Poèmes Arméniens, Anciens et Modernes, Precedés d'une Étude de Gabriel Mourey sur la Poésie et l'Art Arméniens," by Archag Tchobanian, Paris, Librairie A. Charles, 1902; "Chants Populaires Arméniens, Preface de Paul Adam," by Archag Tchobanian, Paris, Société d'Editions Littéraires et Artis- tiques, 1903; "Petite Bibliothèque Arménienne, Publiée sous la Direction de Fréderic Macler," Paris; "L'Orient Inédit, — Legendes et Traditions Armé- niennes," by Minas Tcheraz, Paris, Leroux, 1912; "Études sur la Miniature Arménienne," by Seraphin Abdullah et Frédéric Macler, Paris, 1909; "Au Mi- lieu des Massacres—Journal de la Femme d'un Consul de France en Armé- nie," by Emilie Carlier, Paris, Juven, 1903.

In German: "Die Armenische Literatur," by Franz Nikolaus Finck, Berlin, 1906; "Geschichte der Armenischen Literatur," by Franz Nikolaus Finck, Leipzig, 1909; "Kirchen und Moscheen in Armenian und Kurdistan," Hinrichs, Leipzig, 1913; 71 plates. Maps. Plans.